MUSICIANS INSTITUTE

PRIVATE LESSONS

MODERN ROCK
Rhythm Guitar

A Guide to the Essential Chords, Riffs, Rhythms, and Grooves

by Danny Gill

ISBN 0-634-03982-2

HAL•LEONARD®
CORPORATION

7777 W. BLUEMOUND RD. P.O. BOX 13819 MILWAUKEE, WI 53213

In Australia Contact:
Hal Leonard Australia Pty. Ltd.
22 Taunton Drive P.O. Box 5130
Cheltenham East, 3192 Victoria, Australia
Email: ausadmin@halleonard.com

Copyright © 2003 by HAL LEONARD CORPORATION
International Copyright Secured   All Rights reserved

No part of this publication may be reproduced in any form or
by any means without the prior written permission of the Publisher.

Visit Hal Leonard Online at
www.halleonard.com

Preface

There's an old cliché that says guitarists practice soloing 90 percent of the time and work on rhythm the other 10 percent. In my years of teaching, I've noticed all too frequently that the cliché seems to be true; the majority of time most students spend on the instrument seems to be devoted to lead guitar. As a huge fan of lead guitar, I know that nothing will turn heads more than a great lead player shredding away in the corner of a music store (or a music school for that matter!). The problem is that in the real world of being in a band and playing songs, the guitarist gets to solo at the *most* 10 percent of the time while having to play rhythm the other 90 percent. Look at it this way: while there are a lot of great songs with lousy solos, there has *never* been a great song with a lousy rhythm!

This book is designed to get you started with the techniques and chord knowledge to focus on the main 90 percent of rock music—the rhythm! All you need is a love of this style, a guitar, and a desire to learn. So if you're ready...let's rock!

Credits

Danny Gill: guitar, bass
Soren Fardvik: drums

Recorded at Rubberneck studios by Danny
Drums recorded by Pierre Lysell
Mixed by JanJan Englundh
Photo by Per Stalfors
Thanks to: Max and Alexandra Gill for all of their love (and for listening to all of my music!!)

Contents

Before You Begin...

Before you get started, here are a few tips and suggestions that you might find useful:

1) Rhythm guitar is all about getting in the groove with the rhythm section. So it's a good idea to practice with a metronome or a drum machine in addition to playing along with the CD tracks in this book. Of course, jam with a live rhythm section whenever possible!

2) If you can break a part down and play it slowly, then the speed will come.

3) Since such a huge part of rock rhythm guitar is about tone, I think it's important to practice two ways: with your effects and without. By practicing without effects (distortion, delay, chorus, wah-wah, etc.) you are sure to focus on the intended part. By practicing with your effects, you will have to pay attention to some important techniques such as muting, hand placement, and the control of feedback. You will also have to make some tonal decisions regarding the amount of distortion, pickup selection, etc. After you can play the parts, practice as though you are in a live performance situation.

4) You are your own best teacher. Record yourself, and listen. Use your ears and be objective. If you sound horrible at first there is only one way to go—up!!

5) There are a lot of great rock rhythm guitarists out there. Try to check some of these guys out:

James Hetfield	(Metallica)
Dimebag Darrell	(Pantera)
Dave Mustaine	(Megadeth)
Angus and Malcolm Young	(AC/DC)
Eddie Van Halen	(Van Halen)
Fredrik Thordendal	(Meshuggah)
Nuno Bettencourt	(Extreme)
Adam Jones	(Tool)
Tom Morello	(Rage Against The Machine)
Tony Iommi	(Black Sabbath)
Jimmy Page	(Led Zeppelin)
John Frusciante	(Red Hot Chili Peppers)
Mattias "IA" Eklundh	(Freak Kitchen)
Zakk Wylde	(Ozzy Osbourne)

Also give a closer listen to the rhythm playing of some of your favorite players.

Chapter One
CONTROL YOURSELF

Sixteenth Notes and Power Chords

Let's dive right in and do some jamming! This first groove is based on a sixteenth-note pattern and uses power chords. We'll look more at power chords and sixteenth notes later.

Track 1 Track 2
(slow)

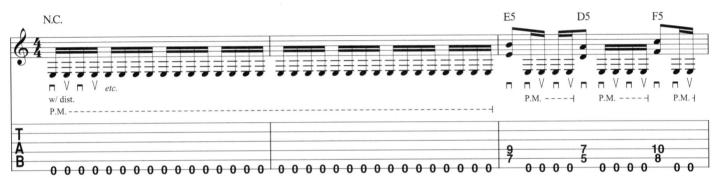

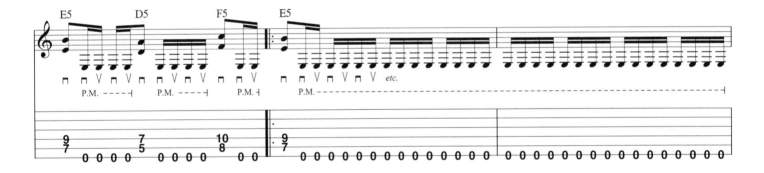

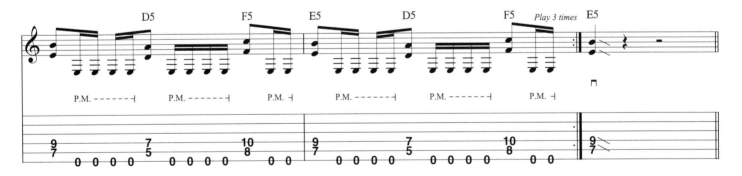

Some basic rules to live by:

- Choke up on the pick. This will give you maximum control.
- When playing at a quick tempo such as in this first example, it's a good idea to rest the side of your picking hand against the bridge of your guitar. This will allow you to mute the strings and control the *dynamics*.

- Keep the time! Tap your foot or some other part of your body. Quarter notes (one tap per beat) should do it. If you can do this, you can play just about anything. If you can't...the rhythm gods will not be kind to you! Keep at it!

- If it feels good, it is good! Strings, picks, amps, guitars...whatever works for you. In general, the heavier the string, the better the tone and the more in tune your rhythms will be. If you use .009's for solos, try .010's if you're playing mainly rhythms. I usually use a heavy (1.0 mm) pick. But for some of the faster metal rhythms, I like to use a thinner (.60) one. Experiment!

- The picking directions indicated in this book are merely suggestions. If you can play Track 1 up to speed using only downstrokes, more power to you!

Now let's add another part to our first example:

Track 3   Track 4
(slow)

Power Chord Inversions

The chords we've been using in these two examples are known as *power chords*. Power chords are two-note chords consisting of a root and a 5th. The simplicity of the root and 5th sounds great with distortion! Power chords are neither major nor minor because they do not have a 3rd.

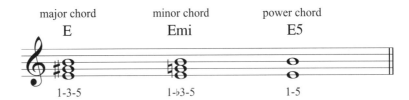

Power chords can be played in two-note forms, as in the previous tracks, or in three-note forms. Three-note forms still contain just the root and 5th, but the root is doubled (an octave higher) for a thicker *voicing*.

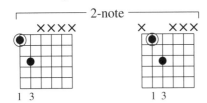   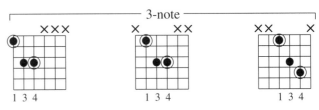

A power chord can also be played as an *inversion*. An inversion exists when any note of a chord other than the root (the 1) is placed in the bass. Since the power chord has only two notes, the 5-1 is the only inversion available. For example, an E power chord contains the root (E) and the 5th (B). To play an inversion of this chord, simply switch the notes around. Put the note B on the bottom and E on the top.

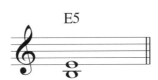

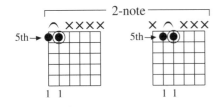   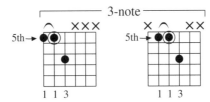   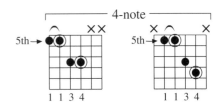

Listen to the difference inversions make. Here's the same example as Track 3, but with inversions on the last four chords:

Track 5

   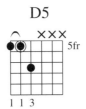   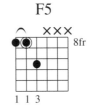   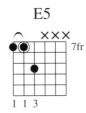

Chapter Two
THE UPS AND DOWNS

2

Accenting Eighth Notes with Open-String Power Chords

Now let's take a look at some different ways we can accent our power chords. A basic rock drum beat looks like this:

In this pattern, the hi-hat plays eighth notes, the kick drum is on beats 1 and 3, and the snare drum is on 2 and 4. The kick and snare are on the *downbeats*. The *upbeats*, which are only sounded by the hi-hat, are placed in between the downbeats. If you're tapping your foot, the downbeat happens when your foot hits the floor. The upbeat will occur when your foot is raised. Here's how to count eighth notes:

count: 1 + 2 + 3 + 4 +

say: "1 and 2 and 3 and 4 and"

Here are some *open-string* power chord shapes you'll need to know for the next few examples:

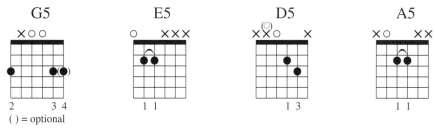

Let's start by accenting on 1 and 3 with the kick drum. Then, we'll begin "scratching" the eighth notes on beats 2 and 4; this helps keep you in the groove. This technique is accomplished by laying your left hand lightly across all six strings to mute them and strumming to produce a deadened "scratch" sound.

Track 6

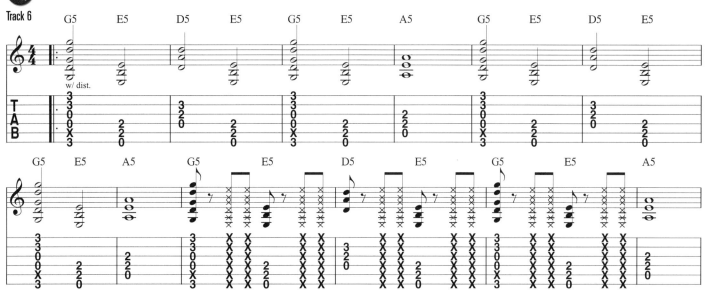

9

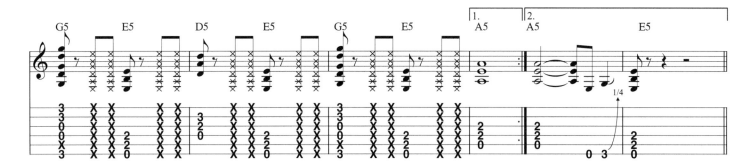

Syncopation

Now let's accent on the upbeat. When the accent is on the upbeat, a rhythm is said to be *syncopated*.

Track 7

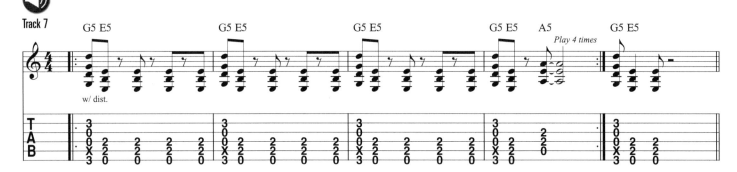

Now we'll move on to the snare drum! This example will accent on beats 2 and 4 with the snare (also known as "the backbeat").

Track 8

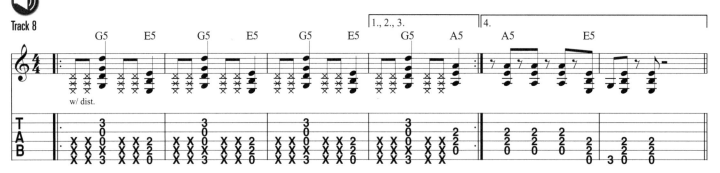

Now the fun begins. Let's combine some of these accents into a song. There are three parts or sections, labeled in the music as A, B, and C. Notice this example starts before the downbeat of beat 1 (where the drums enter). The notes before beat 1 are known as *pickup notes*.

Track 9

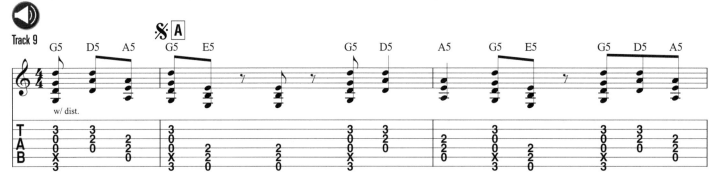

Chapter Three
MUTE-IN-E

3

Muting

Muting gives you control over the dynamics of a song. You can play soft, loud, tight, open, or anything in between. To mute, simply press the side of your picking hand over the strings. The best position for this is usually by the bridge. (Try this whenever you see the abbreviation "P.M.", which stands for "palm muting.")

The amount of pressure you place on the strings with the side of your picking hand is important. If you use too much pressure, the strings will go sharp—too little pressure, and you won't sound "tight" enough. Picking intensity (how hard or soft your picking attack is) also has a lot to do with the dynamics of a muted part. Finding the right balance is what it's all about.

Downstrokes

In the next few examples, we're going to pick using only *downstrokes*. Picking with downstrokes will give you a more consistent picking attack and can sound tighter than alternate picking. This is because the strings are being hit in the same order and from the same angle each time.

Let's start with eighth notes.

Track 10

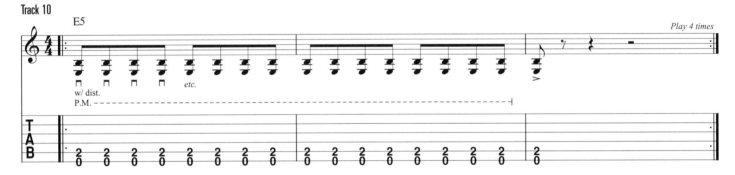

A sixteenth note is when you divide a quarter note into four equal parts:

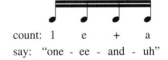

count: 1   e   +   a
say: "one - ee - and - uh"

Here's how it sounds:

Track 11

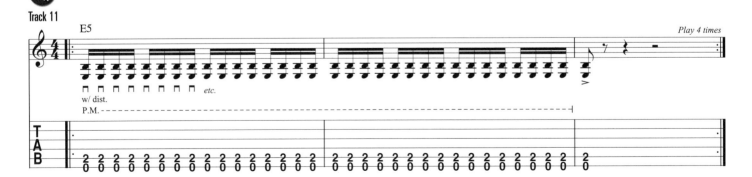

12

Now we'll add a new part and combine eighth notes and sixteenth notes. Pay attention to the dynamics. The song switches from muted to loud, unmuted chords.

Track 12

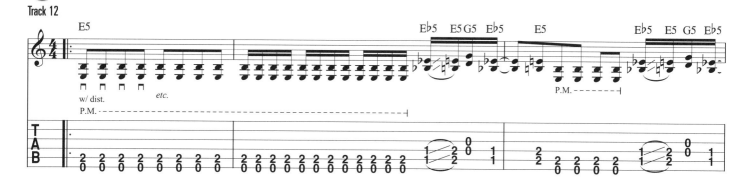

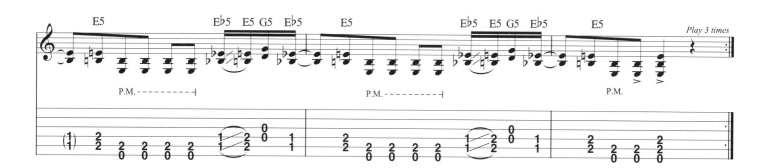

Here's the same riff with accents on some of the upbeats.

Track 13

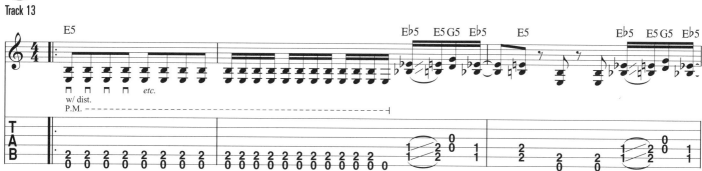

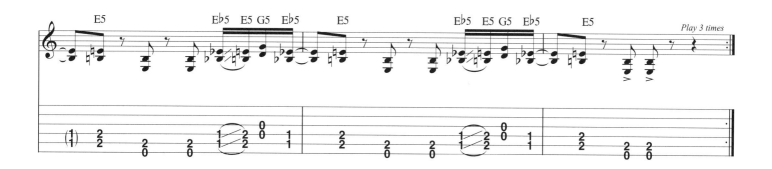

Sixteenth-Note Accents

Now let's try accenting some of the various sixteenth notes. First the "e":

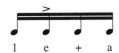

1   e   +   a

Track 14

Here's how that sounds:

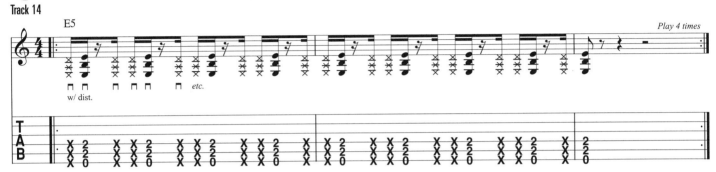

Here's how this sixteenth-note accent can sound when applied to Track 12. Once again, we're accenting the second sixteenth note.

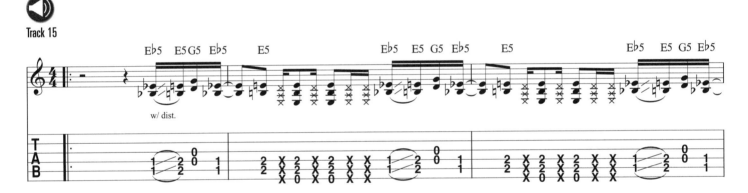

Track 15

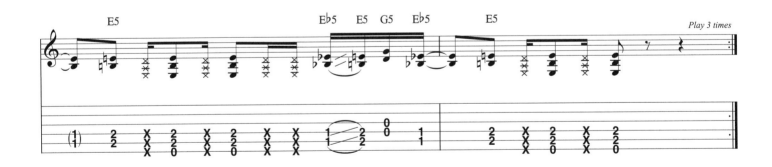

We'll end this chapter with one more variation on this theme. Here the accent is on the "and" (the third sixteenth note).

Track 16

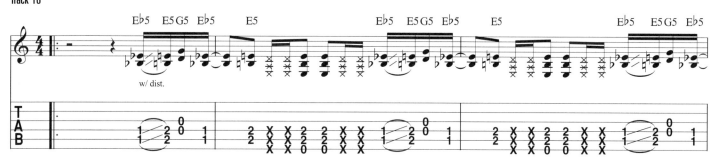

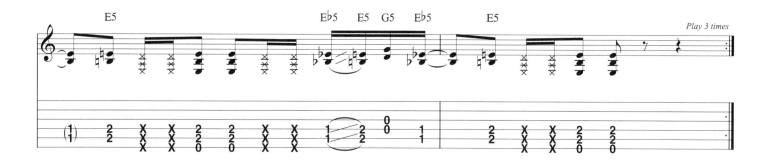

Chapter Four

4

THE BIG THREE

Major and Minor Triads

So far, we've had a great rhythmic workout with the two-note power chord. Now we're going to add the three-note *triad* to our arsenal. There are two main types of triads: major and minor. The chords are built as follows:

The major triad: 1–3–5
The minor triad: 1–♭3–5

For more on the theory of building chords, you can jump to the end of the book (see Chord Theory: By the Numbers). For now, we're going to move ahead with the application of these chords.

Inversions

Earlier in the book we talked about inversions with power chords. Here, we'll be looking at inversions of triads.

A *root position* triad will have the root in the bass.
A *first inversion* triad will have the 3rd in the bass.
A *second inversion* triad will have the 5th in the bass.

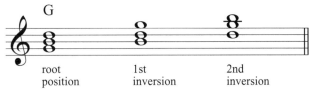

In this chapter (and throughout the book), we will be using root position chords as well as inversions.

Since there are three notes in a triad ("the big three"), you should know how to play both major and minor triads on every set of three strings. Know where the root is at all times! In the following diagrams, the root note is circled. I've chosen the key of G here because it lays out well on the fretboard, but these shapes are movable to any key (as you'll soon see).

G Major Triad Shapes

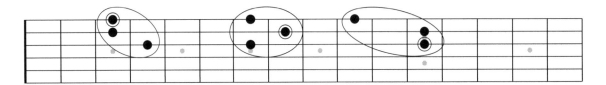

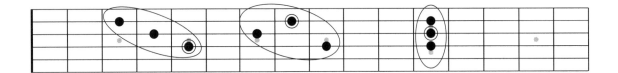

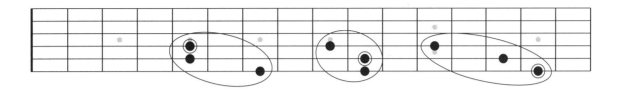

G Minor Triad Shapes

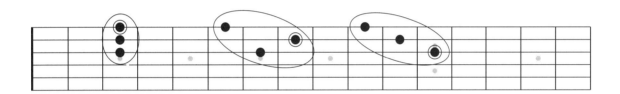

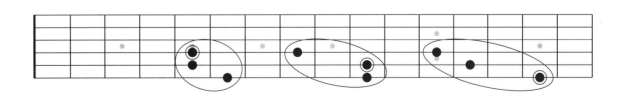

It also helps if you can see the three-note shapes as part of these bigger triad voicings, with which you may already be familiar. (If not, get familiar with them!)

Major

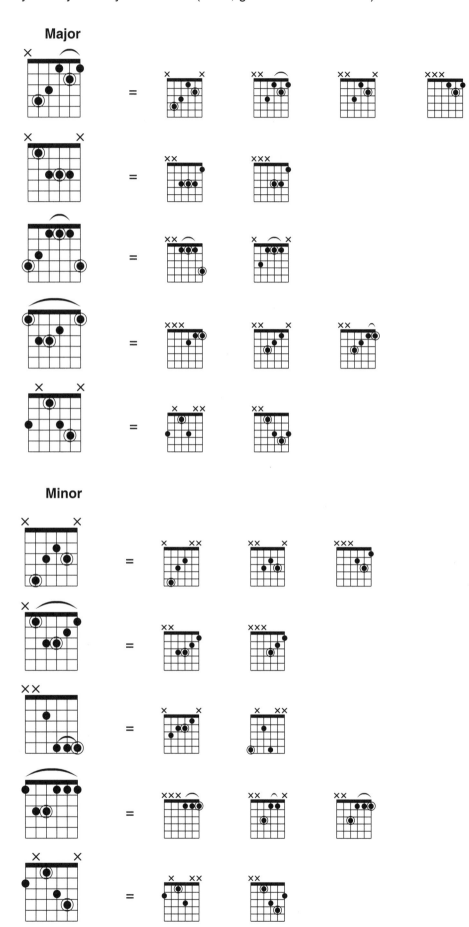

Minor

This next exercise combines A major triad shapes in three octaves. Play through #1–8 consecutively

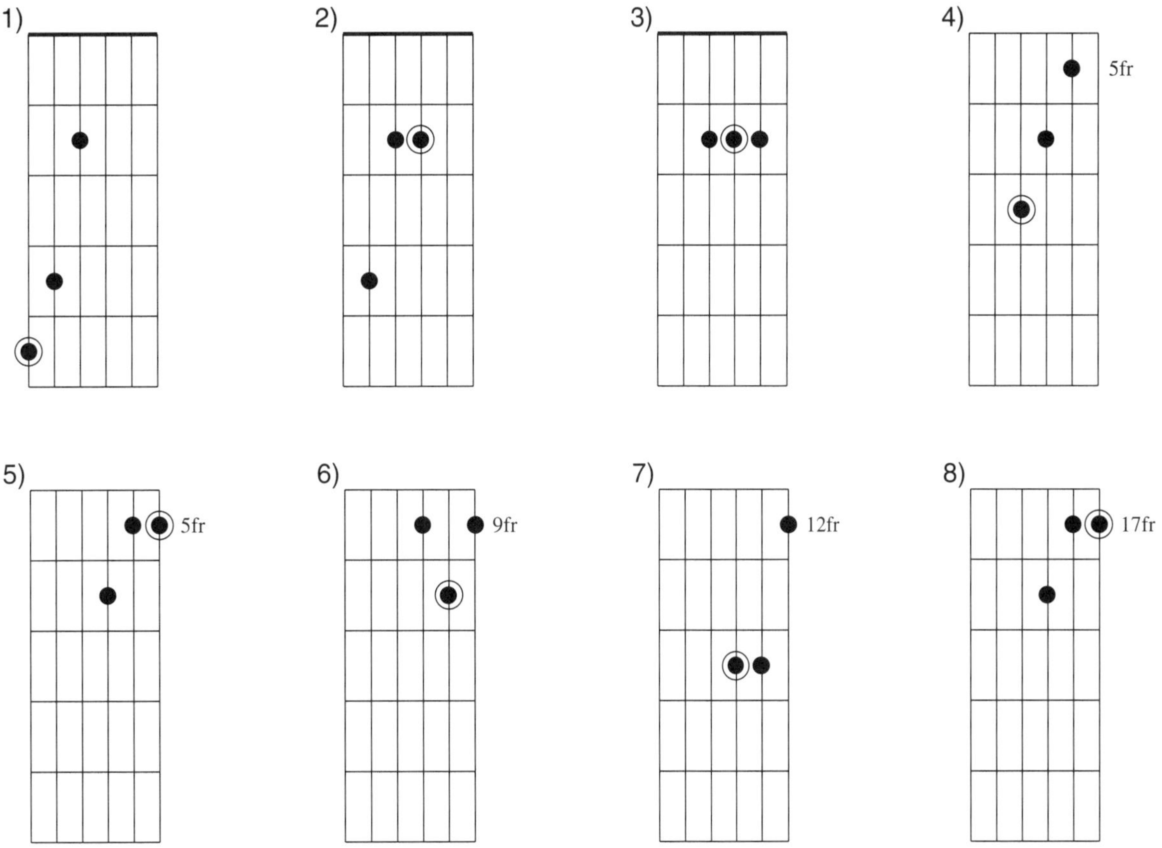

1)

2)

3)

4) 5fr

5) 5fr

6) 9fr

7) 12fr

8) 17fr

Here we see the A minor triad shapes in three octaves.

1)

2)

3)

4) 5fr

5) 5fr

6) 8fr

7) 12fr

8) 17fr

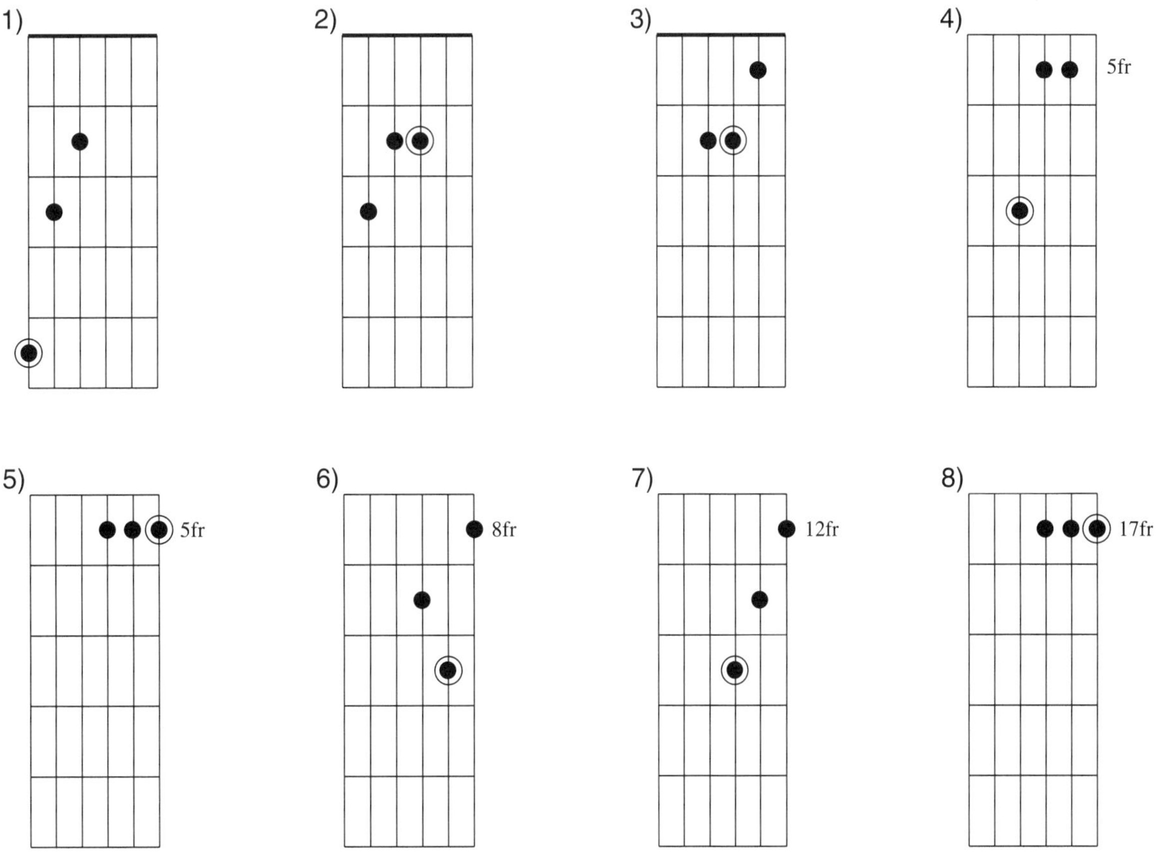

The main reason to learn all of these shapes is to give you some harmonic and textural variety in your rhythms, even when playing the same three chords! Here's a simple jam in A to get you started with some of these shapes.

Note: In chord charts, inversions are commonly written as *slash chords*. For example, the symbol G/B indicates a G chord with B in the bass.

Track 17

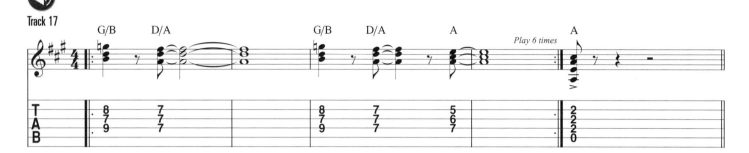

This next example also uses the chords A, G, and D, but takes you down the neck from tenth position to open position.

Track 18

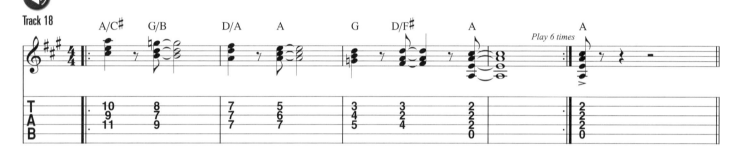

Now here's a tricky one in A. The chords switch fast, so you'll have to be ready!

Track 19

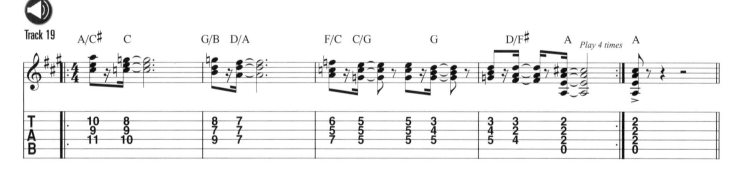

Now let's use some triads on the top three strings. We'll start off easy in D. Notice the D bass note in each chord. This drone makes each chord sound nice and fat.

Track 20

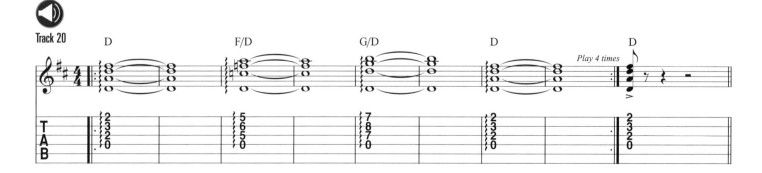

Now let's add a few more chords:

Track 21

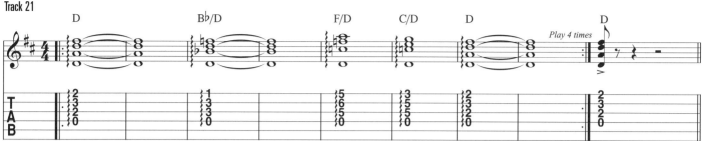

Here's a longer example using triads on the top three strings. The basic strumming rhythm is shown above the chord symbols to help you get started.

Note: I use Drop D tuning for this one so I can play the sixth string as a drone. It helps, but it's not necessary. We're going to get into Drop D tuning in Chapter 7.

Track 22

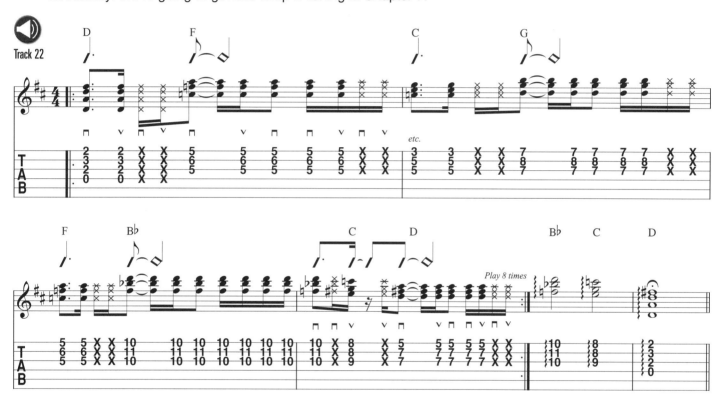

Now let's add a minor triad into the mix. Here's the basic progression:

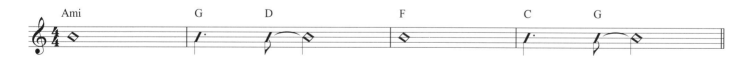

Now test yourself. If you know your triads, you should be able to play this tune in at least twelve places on the neck (three positions on each set of three strings, plus any combination)! Some possibilities are shown on the next page. Pay close attention to where the root of each chord is.

On bottom three strings:

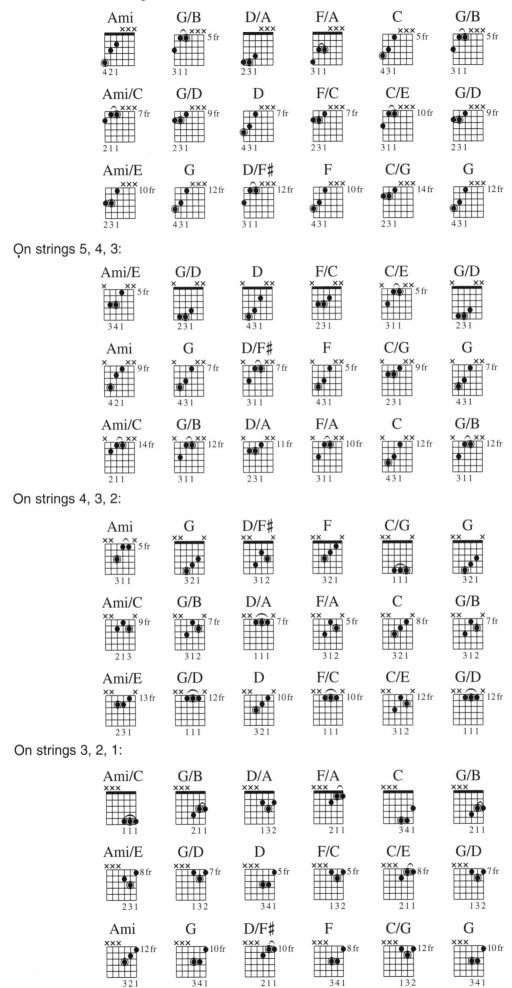

On strings 5, 4, 3:

On strings 4, 3, 2:

On strings 3, 2, 1:

This example uses the 4–3–2 string group:

Track 23

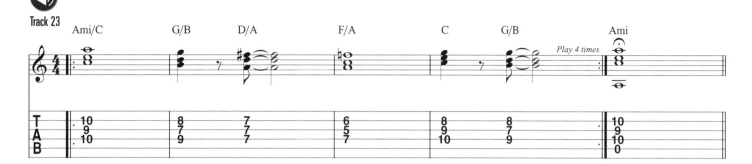

Chord "Bits"

We don't always need to play all three notes to imply the quality of a triad. One of my favorite sounds is using only the 3rd in the bass and the root note on top.

Track 24

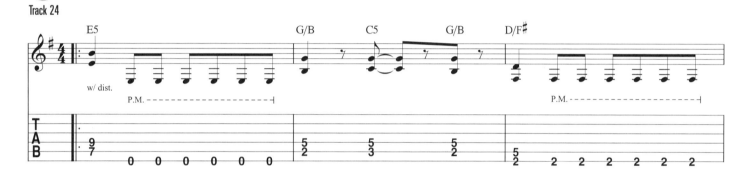

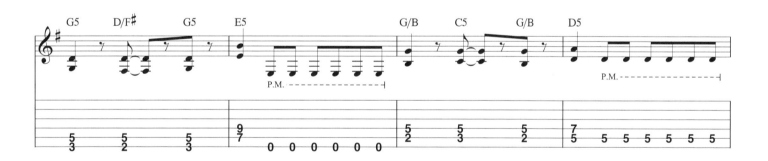

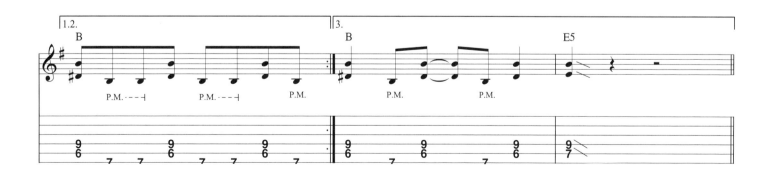

Chapter Five
MAIDEN VOYAGE (IN THE BEGINNING)

Sometime in the early eighties, there was a popular musical movement known as "The New Wave of British Heavy Metal". These bands laid the groundwork for a lot of metal bands that were to follow in the mid to late eighties, including Metallica, Def Leppard, and Megadeth. Metallica even paid tribute to a lot of TNWOBHM bands on their *Garage Days* albums. One of the most influential bands defining this sound was Iron Maiden. Among other things, they are known for this rhythm:

Track 25

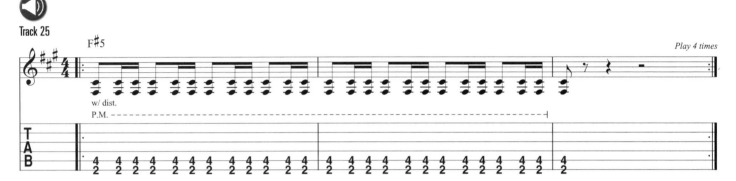

Although they didn't invent this rhythm, they certainly sold a lot of records with it. Get familiar with it, as this little seed of a riff can grow into a monster! It also sounds a lot like Black Sabbath in the Dio era.

Now let's add some more chords. Notice some of the chord changes are on the "e" (the second sixteenth note):

Track 26

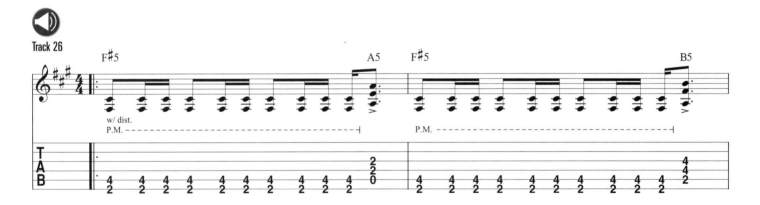

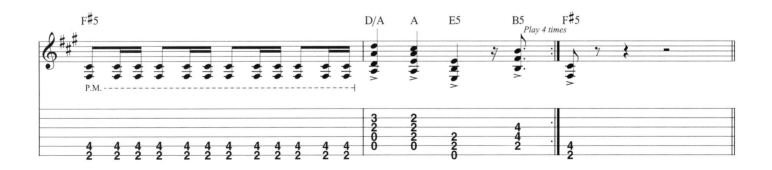

The Fox Trot

If we speed up this rhythm, we get the famous "fox trot":

Track 27

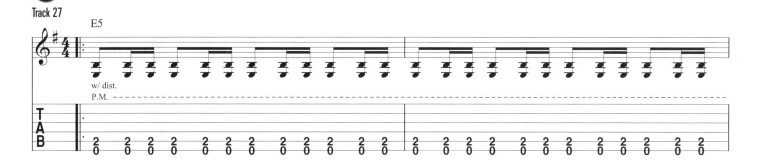

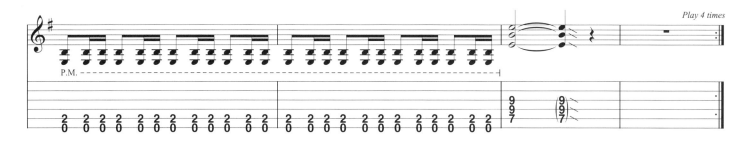

Now let's add some chords. Notice the alternating voicings on the C and D chords. Let's put some of our inversions to work!

Track 28

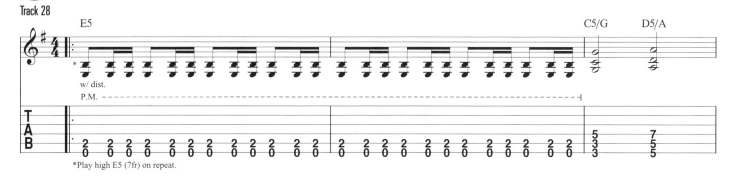

*Play high E5 (7fr) on repeat.

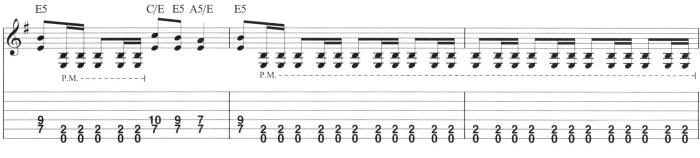

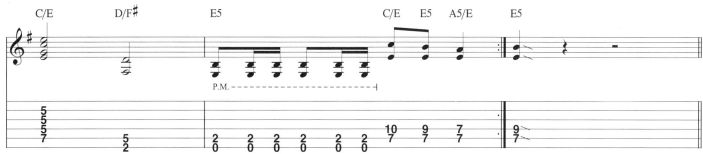

This one's a little tough. The C/E chord will require a bit of a stretch. While the chords ring, see if you can keep the rhythm chugging on the low strings.

Track 29

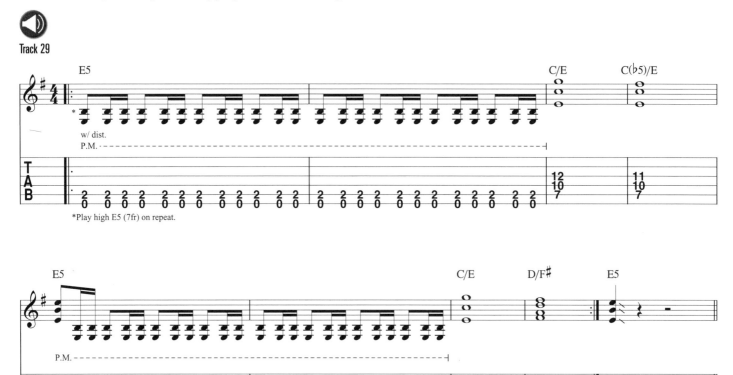

*Play high E5 (7fr) on repeat.

Combining Eighths and Sixteenths

By combining different rhythms, all sorts of possibilities open up. Here we move some of the sixteenth notes around:

Track 30

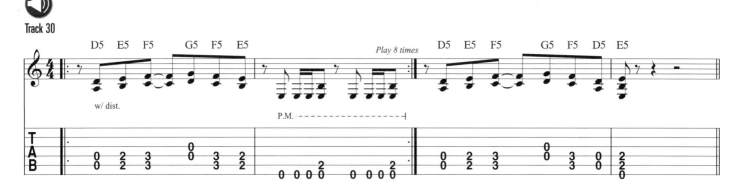

There are lots of variations. Check out a few more:

Track 31

And finally, let's add a chord to see how these different rhythmic accents sound in context:

Track 34

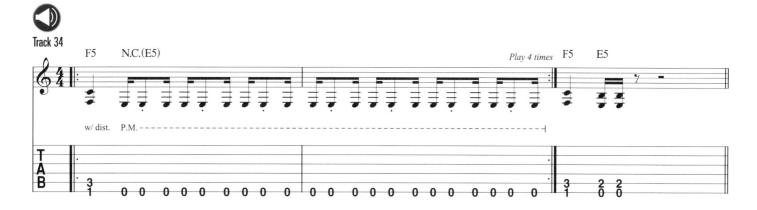

Chapter Six
PICK UP THE PACE

So far we've done a lot of work subdividing a beat into eighth notes and sixteenth notes. Two other common subdivisions are *sextuplets* and *thirty-second notes*.

Sextuplets

A *sextuplet* occurs when a quarter note (one beat) is divided into six equal parts.

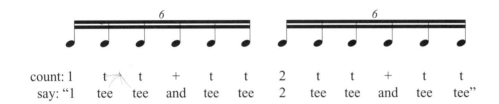

One of my teachers at MI (who may wish to remain anonymous) also taught me a good trick. Say "bottle in front of me, frontal lobotomy" when counting sextuplets. Both work. I think the first may be a little more "correct"!

Here's what they sound like:

Track 35

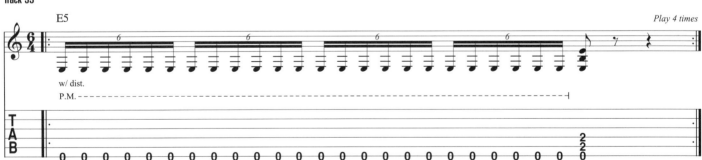

It's a little tougher if we switch notes. Keep the right hand going!

Track 36

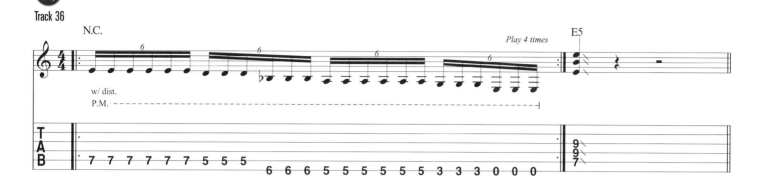

The sextuplets don't have to be constant. Mixing up the rhythms will give your riffs some space and should help them groove. Here we add some quarter notes to a sextuplet riff:

Track 37

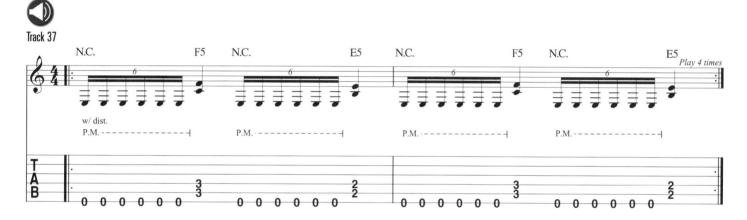

Now let's combine the previous two riffs into one:

Track 38

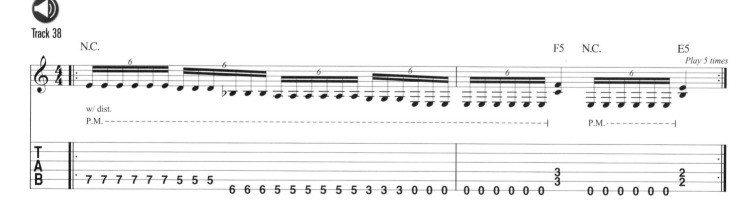

The sextuplet itself can be divided in a lot of ways. Here's one possibility:

Track 39

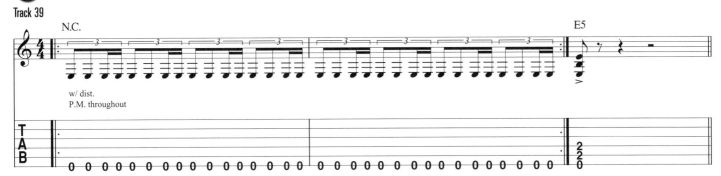

Here's how it can sound in context:

Track 40

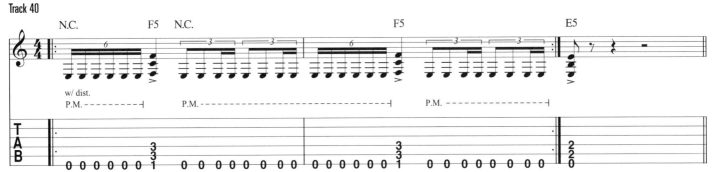

Let's take a look at a few more ways to divide up the sextuplet:

Track 41

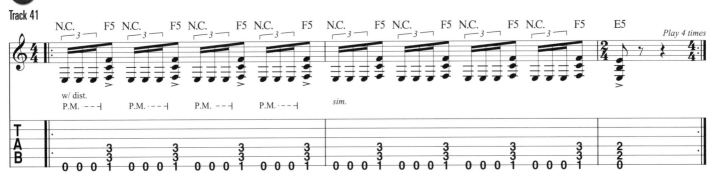

Track 42

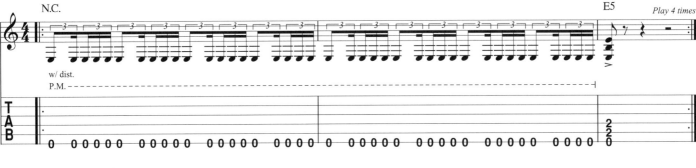

Let's put these rhythms to work. Here's how the previous two riffs can sound in context. This riff also includes some sliding octaves.

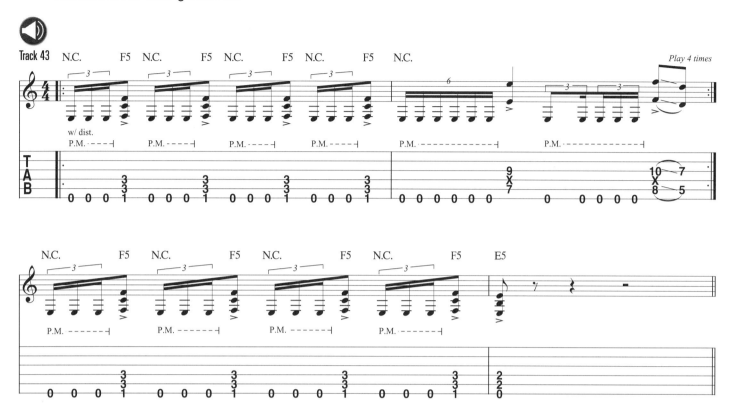

And here's one more variation for good luck:

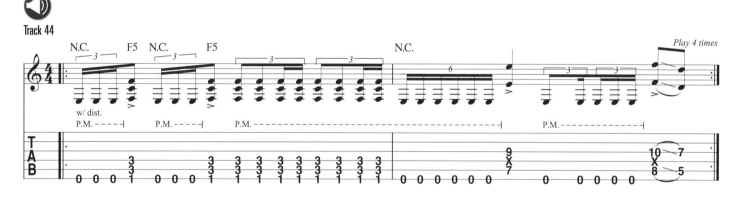

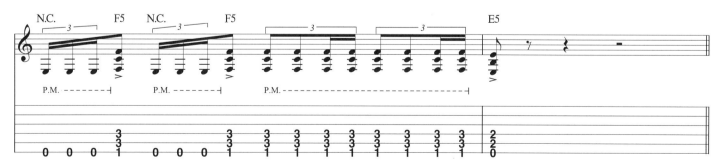

Thirty-Second Notes

A thirty-second note occurs when the quarter note is divided into eight equal parts.

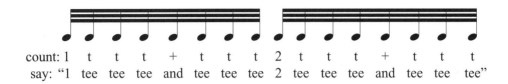

count: 1 t t t + t t t 2 t t t + t t t
say: "1 tee tee tee and tee tee tee 2 tee tee tee and tee tee tee"

Let's start on an F♯:

Track 45

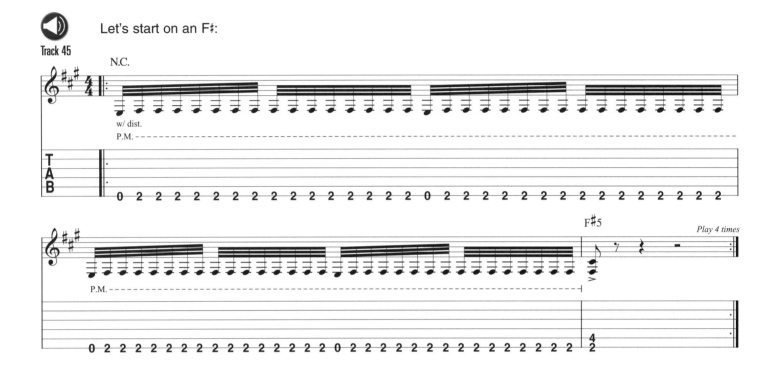

Now let's add a few more notes:

Track 46

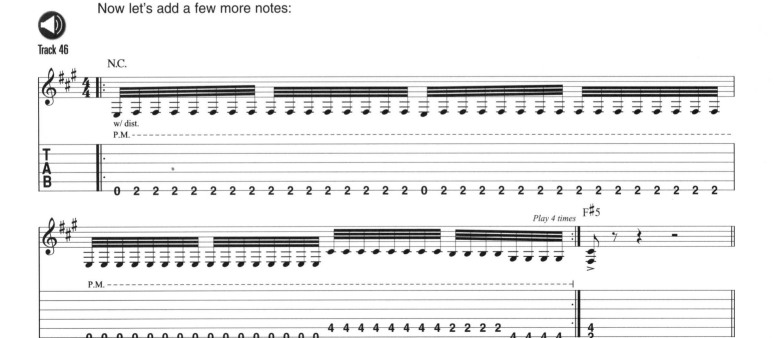

And now let's break it up with a few chords:

Track 47

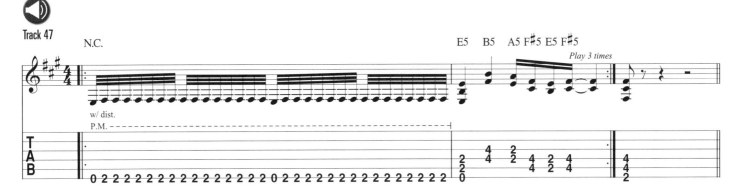

Now that you've built up your thirty-second notes, it's time to break 'em down! Here are a few possibilities:

Track 48

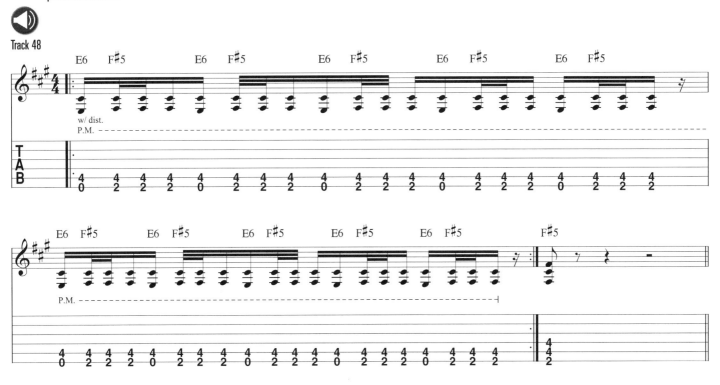

Now we'll add some chords:

Track 49

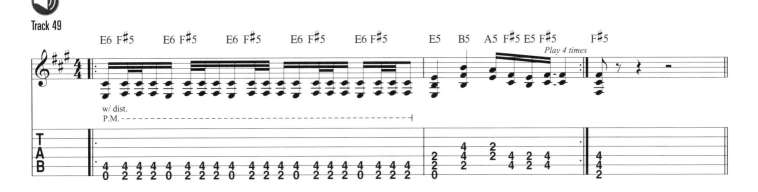

Here are a few more variations to practice:

Track 50

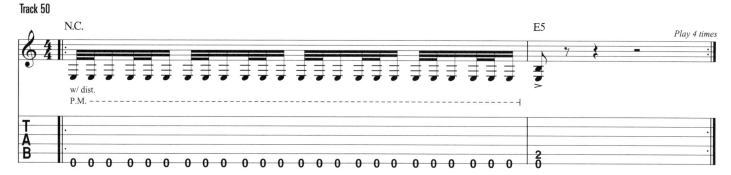

Track 51

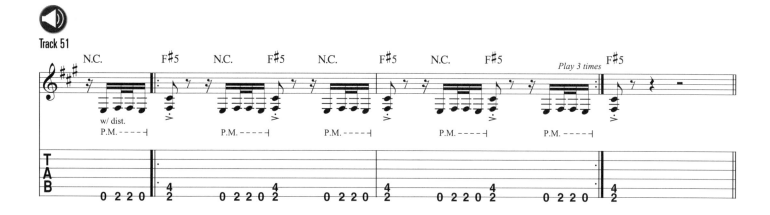

Track 52

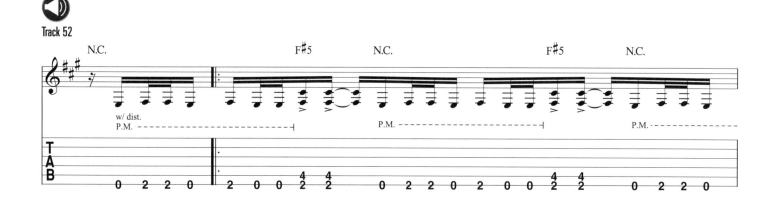

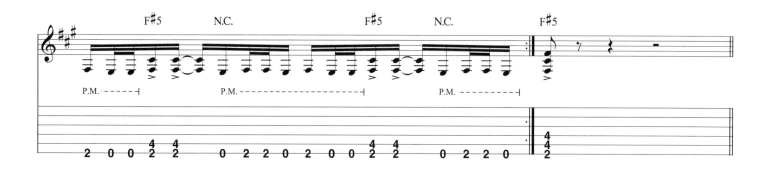

Track 53

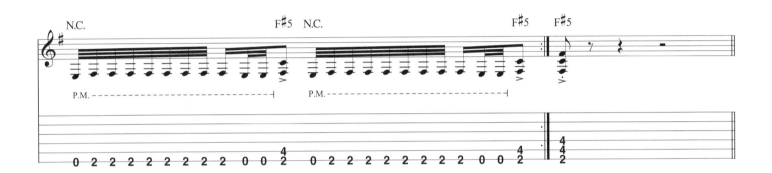

Now that we've got our sixteenth-note triplets and our thirty-second notes happening, why not put 'em together? It's tough, but it sounds great!

Track 54

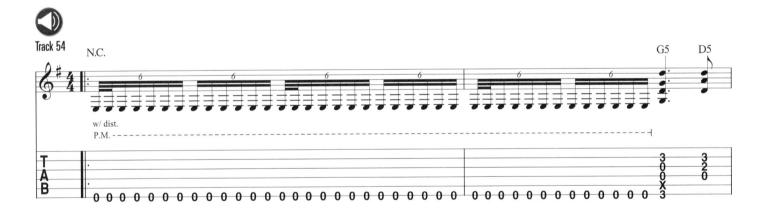

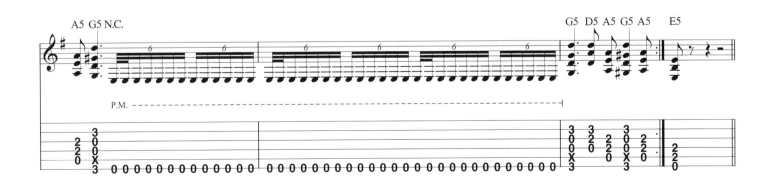

Track 55

Just in case that wasn't enough thirty-second notes, here's a few more!

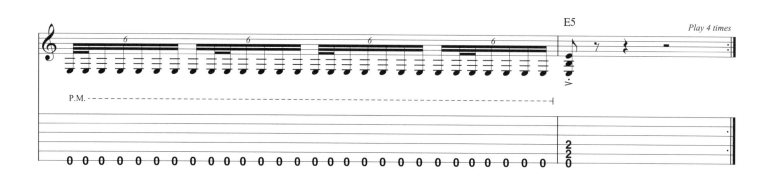

And for the end-of-chapter challenge, let's add some chords to the previous riff:

Track 56

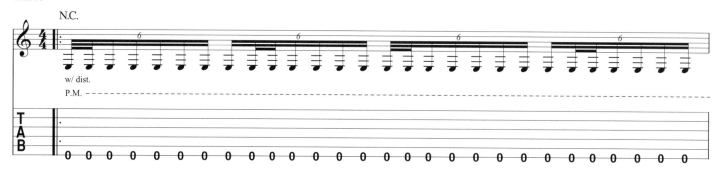

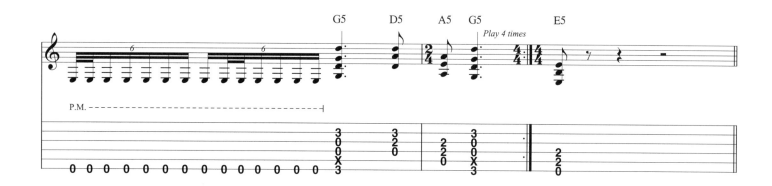

Chapter Seven
D-TUNED

7

It's hard to believe we've made it this far into the book without talking about Drop D tuning! Since around 1990, it seems that more bands tune their guitar with Drop D than with standard tuning. Almost every rock band I can think of has recorded at least a few songs this way.

The Tuning

The concept is very simple: tune your low E (sixth) string down a whole step to D. That's it! Here's how the guitar should be tuned:

(low to high) D–A–D–G–B–E

There are a lot of cool things that can happen now that we've got two D strings. For one thing, we can play a power chord simply by hitting the bottom two, or even bottom three strings!

Track 57

It's important to remember what the chord names are now that we are tuned differently. Let's add a few more chords to our previous example:

Track 58

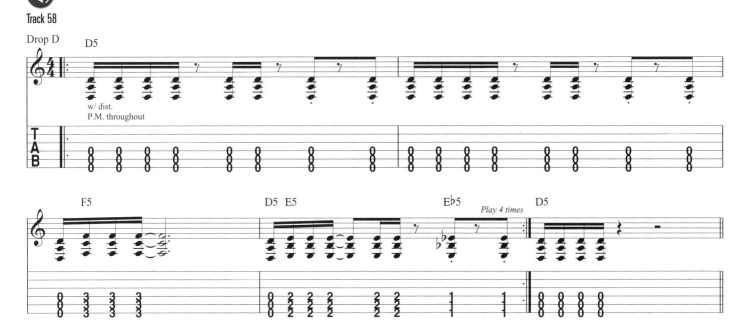

37

Track 59

Here's one more example using this same chord shape:

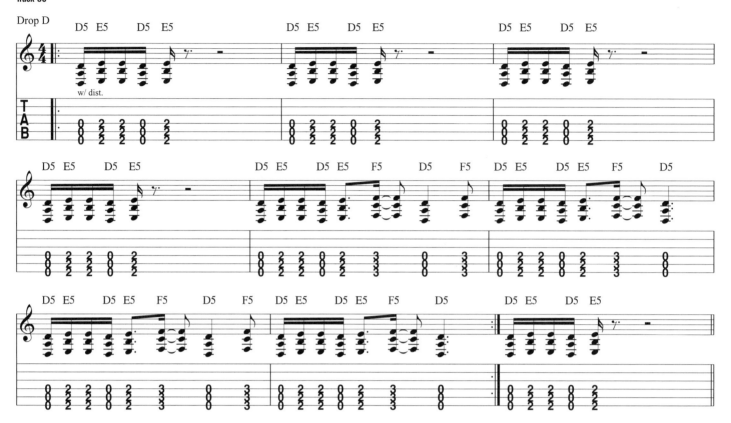

We can also add the G string and the B string to get some big five-string power chords:

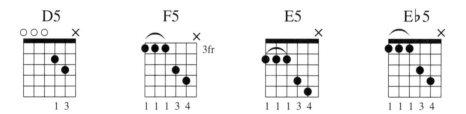

Track 60

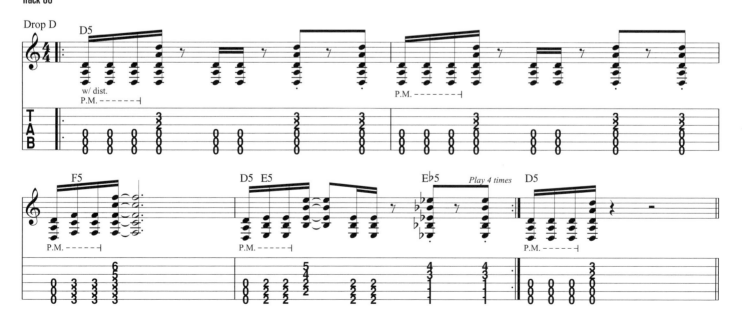

This tuning gives you a lot of cool picking patterns in D that are not possible in standard tuning. Here's an example

Track 61

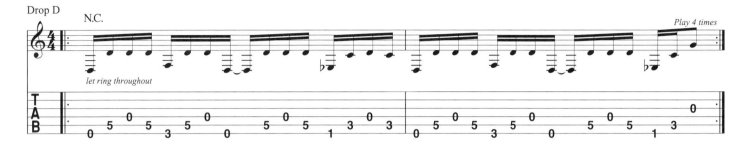

Not-So-Common Chords

Now that we can play a power chord with one finger, our other fingers are free to add some scale tones to this basic shape. These chords would be a lot more difficult in standard tuning!

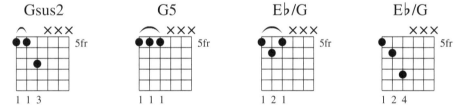

Track 62

Check out what you can do with these shapes while staying in one position:

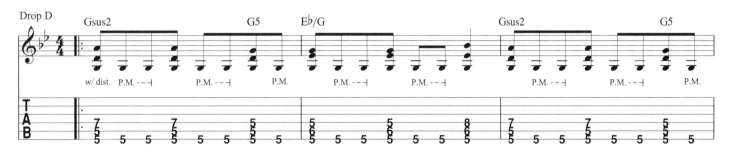

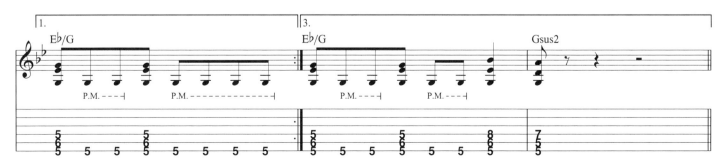

And if we move around a bit:

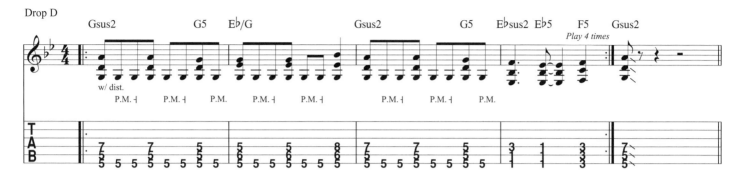

For the final jam in this chapter, we're going to take this idea a bit further. With Drop D tuning, there are some very interesting voice leading possibilities on the bottom strings:

Track 64

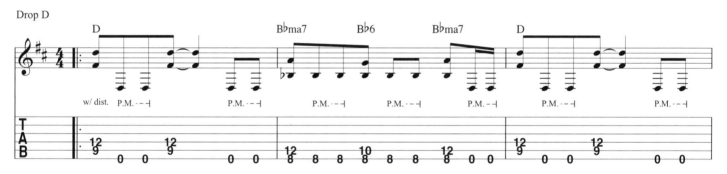

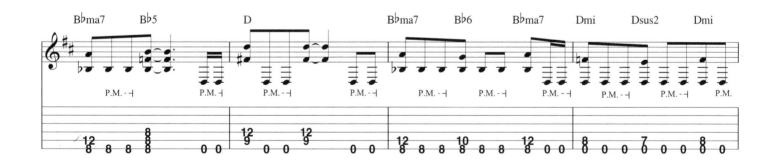

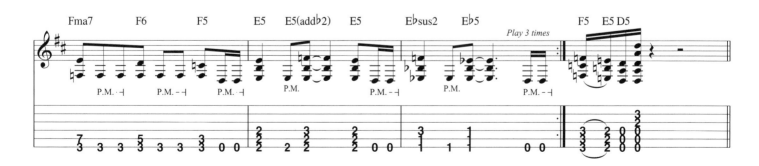

Chapter Eight
ODDS AND ENDS

S o far, the examples in this book have been in 4/4 time. This is also known as *common time*, because 4/4 is by far the most common time signature in rock, as well as most other forms of western music.

Odd Meters

An *odd meter* is any time signature that is *not* 4/4, or common time. Odd meters may be a little difficult at first, but the effort is well worth it. A whole other world awaits!

Let's break it down. When looking at a piece of music, the time signature appears just after the clef sign. The top number represents the *amount* of notes in a measure. The bottom number represents the type of note.

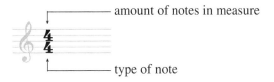

For example, in 4/4 time, the top "4" indicates there are four notes in each measure. The bottom "4" indicates that the quarter note receives one beat.

In 3/4 time, each measure will add up to three quarter notes. Here's an example in 3/4:

Track 65

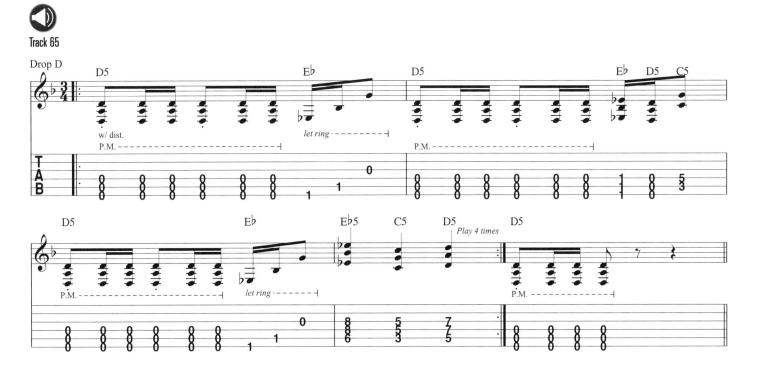

In 5/4, each measure will add up to five quarter notes.

Track 66

Drop D

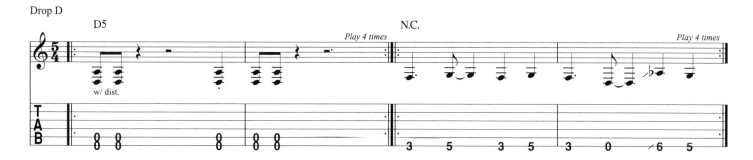

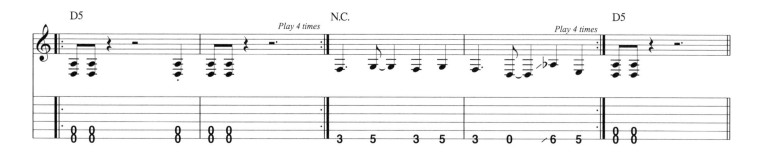

6/4 time will have a total of six quarter notes per measure. (Notice we're back in standard tuning for this one.)

Track 67

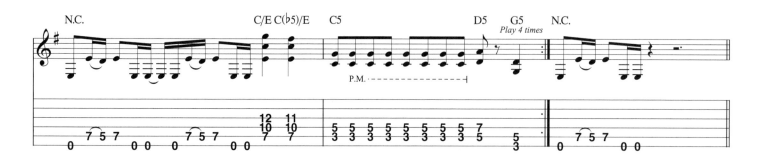

7/4 will have—you guessed it—seven quarter notes per measure.

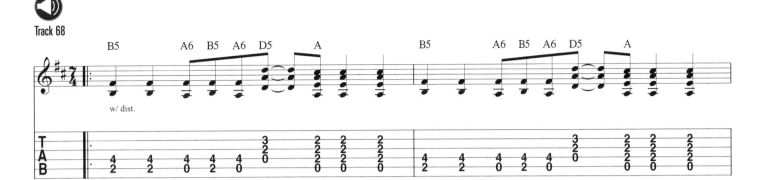

Track 68

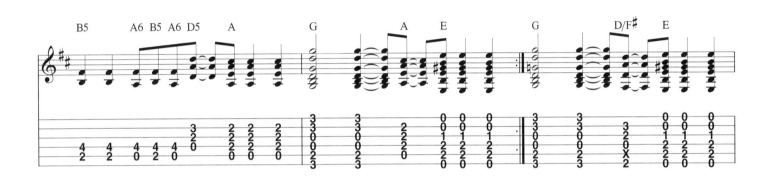

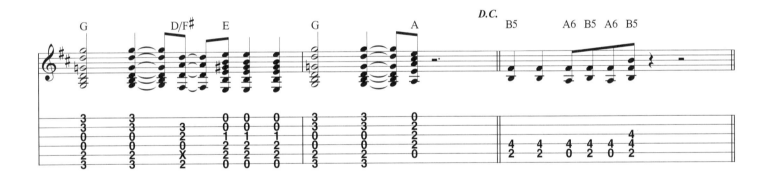

Not all rhythms use the quarter note as the basic subdivision. Another common subdivision is the eighth note. For example, in 6/8 each measure will add up to six eighth notes. (Note: Although a measure of 3/4 time also adds up to six eighth notes, the underlying pulse in 6/8 will be the eighth note. In 3/4 the underlying pulse is the quarter note.)

Don't forget to tune down for this one!

Track 69

Drop D

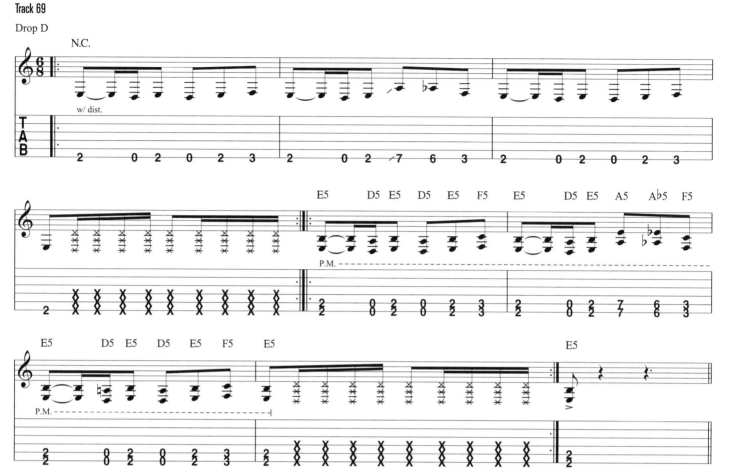

Shufflin' On

The *shuffle* is based on a triplet rhythm with the middle note missing. Here's how to play it: start by playing three notes per beat. Now take out the middle note, leaving only the first and the third. That's it!

The shuffle can be written two different ways: in 12/8 and 4/4. In 12/8 time, there will be twelve eighth notes in one measure.

Shuffle rhythms are often written in 4/4 because they are easier to read than 12/8! The indication to play 4/4 time with a shuffle feel looks like this:

Here's what this sounds like. You've probably heard a groove like this before!

Track 70

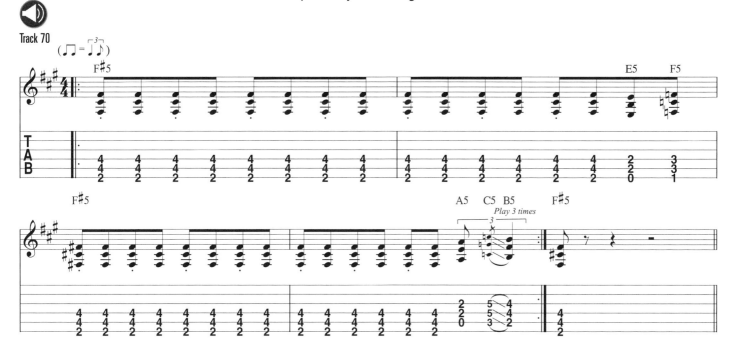

Track 71

The shuffle also sounds great at a quicker tempo:

3+3+2 Rhythm

A great way to really accent a part is to use the *3+3+2 rhythm.* This is a common syncopation that can be played across four beats or across two beats:

Track 72

Here's how it sounds:

Track 73

Here's a little longer example:

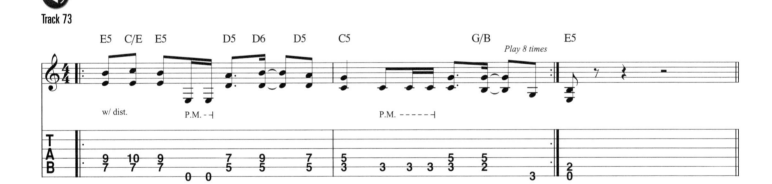

Swing Feel

A *swing* groove is written the same as a straight groove. The difference is more in how you *feel* the rhythm. The second and fourth sixteenth notes are slightly delayed. The indication to play sixteenth notes with a swing feel looks like this:

Track 74

Here's how it sounds:

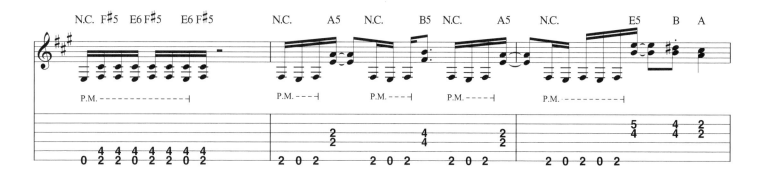

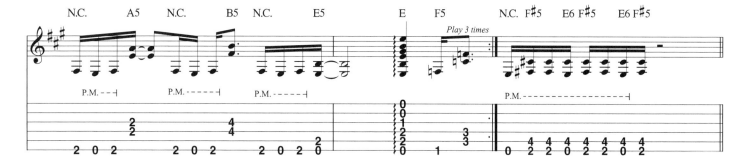

Chapter Nine
OFF THE BEATEN PATH

9

The time has come to add some new chords to your collection! Here are some of my personal favorites.

The Add♯11 Chord

E5(add♯11)

I love the sound of this chord! The formula for this chord is 1–5–♯11. Although there is no 3rd in the chord, the ♯11 will resolve to a major 3rd in our next example. For more on the theory of any chord presented in this chapter, check out the end of the book.

Track 75

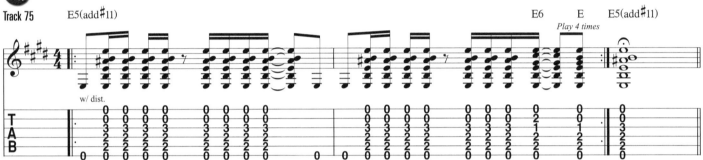

The 7#9 Chord

No self-respecting rock guitarist can live without the "Hendrix" chord! This chord is technically known as the 7♯9. The formula is 1–3–5–♭7–♯9. We'll groove on an E7(♯9) with the root on the A string:

Track 76

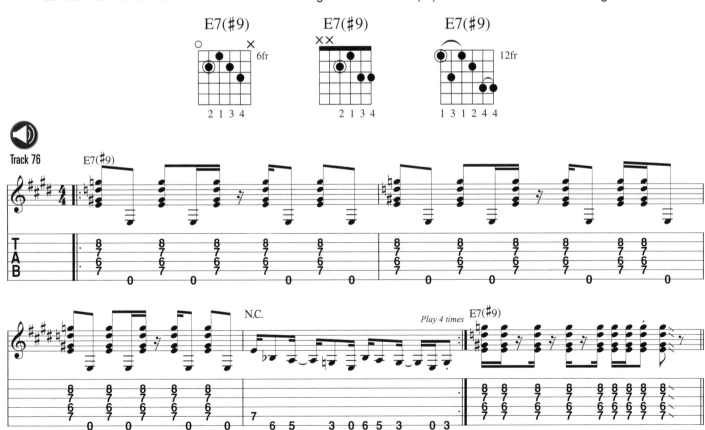

The Minor Add9 Chord

Another one of my favorites is the minor add9 chord. This is a minor triad with a 9th added. The formula is 1–♭3–5–9.

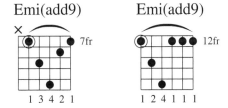

Our next example uses an Emi(add9) chord and a Cadd9(#11) chord. The formula we're using for the add9(#11) is 1–5–9–#11.

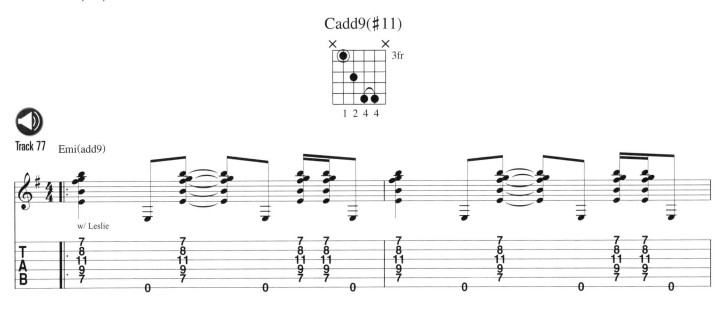

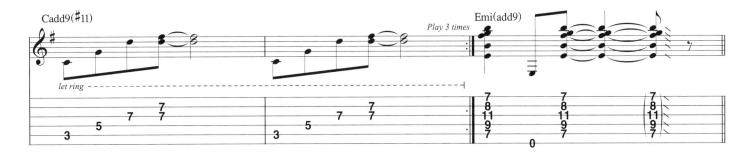

The Sus4 Chord

Another chord we hear all the time is the suspended 4th chord, more commonly known as the sus4. The sus4 chord is neither major nor minor because it does not contain a 3rd. The formula for the sus4 chord is 1–4–5.

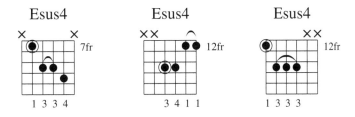

The suspension is almost always followed by a resolution. The resolution can be major or minor. This next example uses both:

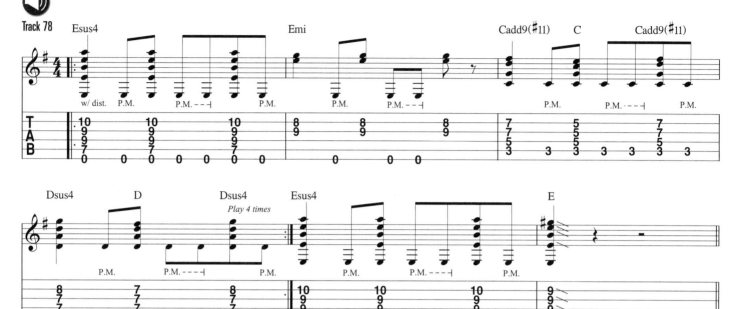

The Sus2 Chord

We can also suspend the 2nd. The formula for a sus2 chord would be 1–2–5. The sus2 can also be called *add9(no 3rd)* or even *power add2* (which would be written E5/2, for example). There are often many ways to write out the same chord.

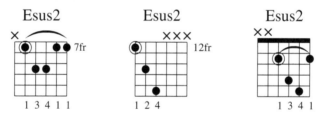

This next example combines the sus2 with some *open-string chords*. Using open strings can provide some lush textures; i.e., they sound cool, dude!

More Open-String Chords

Here is a harmonized E major scale using the open B and E strings. The chord names get a little strange with the open strings, so I've only written the *implied* sound of each chord. Try doing this in other keys!

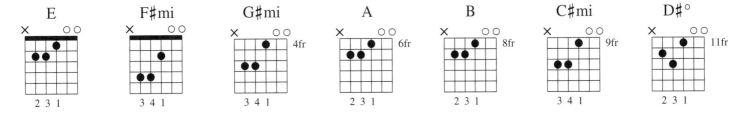

Here's another one of my favorites—F#11. It doesn't sound the same in any other key!

Track 80

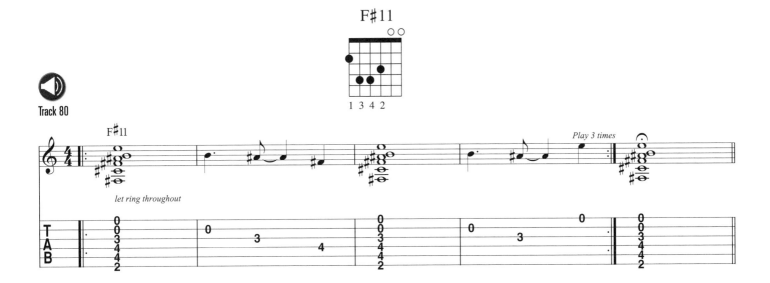

The Single-Note Riff

We could spend a whole book on this. The idea is to come up with a single-note line that serves as the main body or riff of a song. This has a bluesy feel in A.

Track 81 (slow)   Track 82 (fast)

Harmonics

This is the one to impress your friends and neighbors with. Here we're adding some natural open-string harmonics to a basic chord progression. It's a very refreshing sound.

Track 83

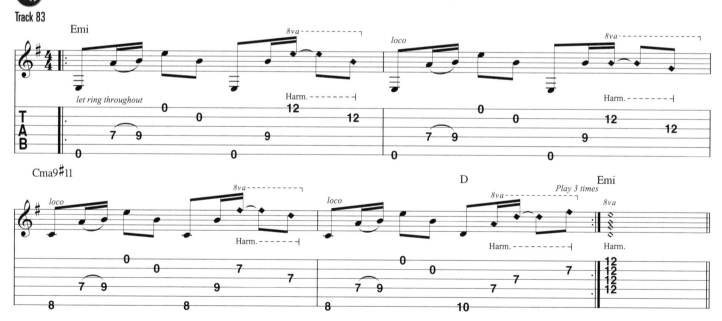

This is certainly a short list of ideas. There are an infinite number of chords, voicings, inversions, and combinations of notes to experiment with. These are just a few I like that I think are pretty useful. When you come up with some that you like, be sure to write them down or record them so you don't forget them!

Chapter Ten
JAM TRACK

 Our final CD track is a full song that utilizes many of the ideas and concepts presented in this book. Here's what's involved:

- **Time changes**   The song starts in 4/4. It then changes to 3/4 and finally ends up in a shuffle groove.
- **Rhythmic variation**   This song has all of the rhythmic values we've talked about: quarter notes, eighth notes, sixteenth notes, thirty-second notes, and even quarter-note triplets.
- **Drop D tuning**   We'll be tuning down for this one.
- **Chord shapes**   You're going to be using triad inversions, #11 chords, add9 chords, and a few more.

Crank it up, and good luck!!

Track 84

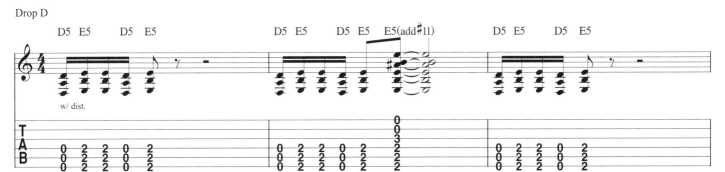

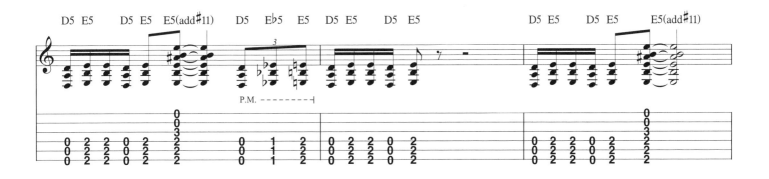

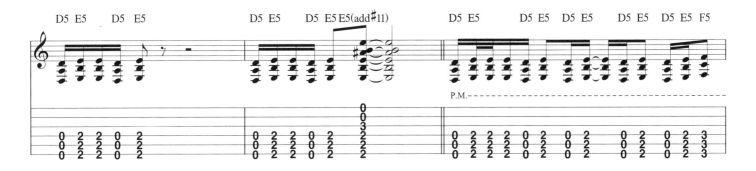

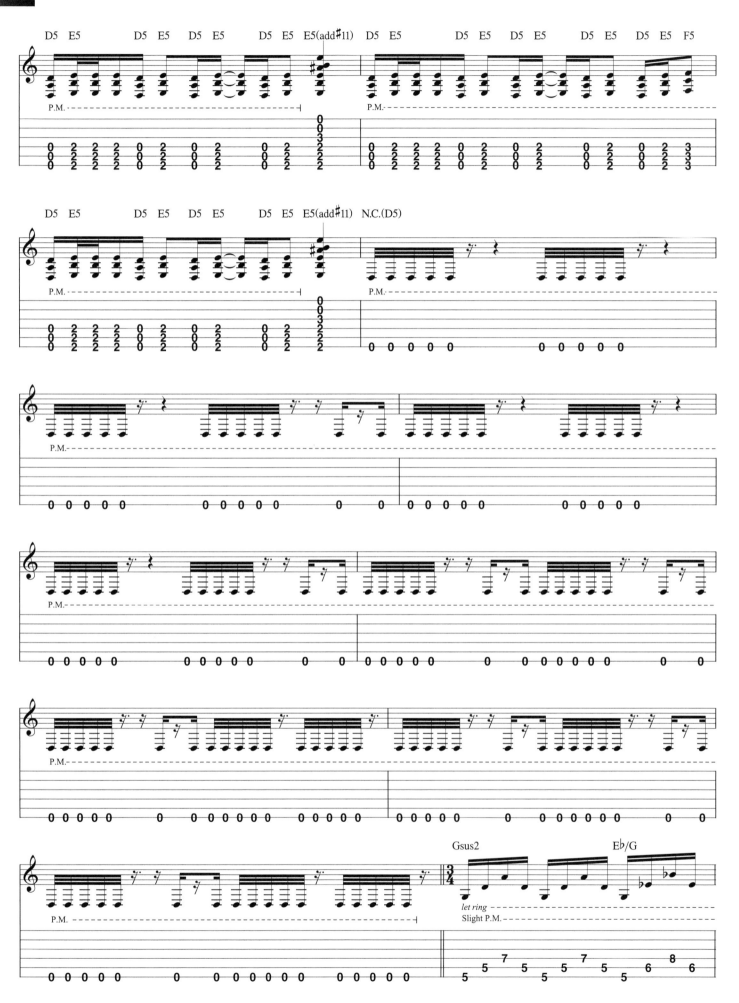

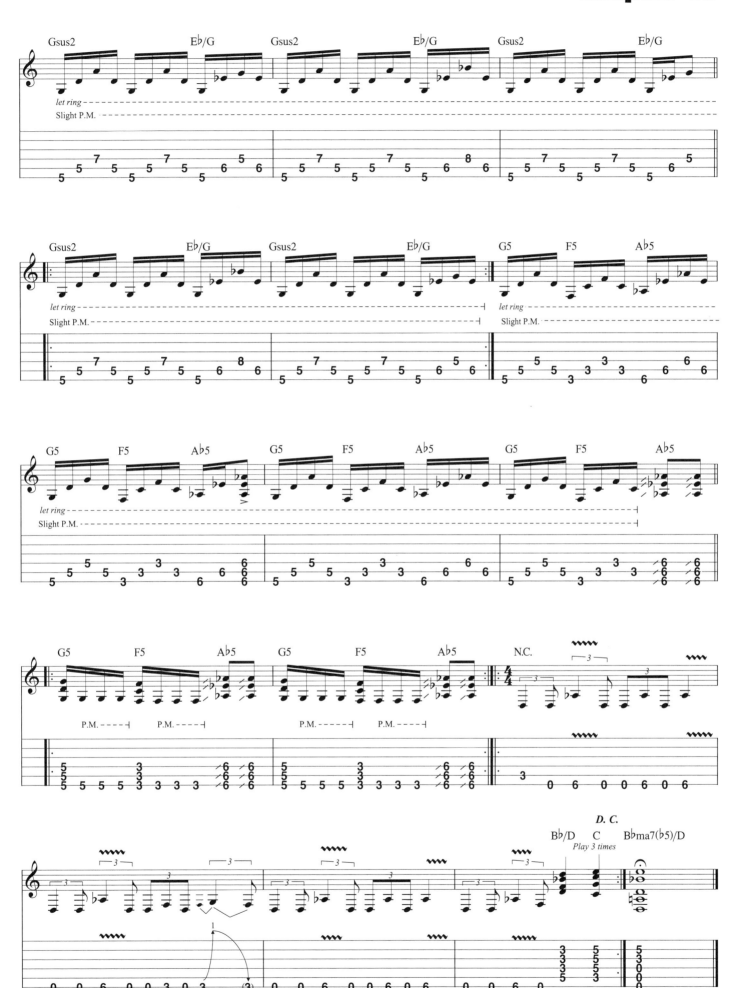

Chord Theory
BY THE NUMBERS

If you've made it through this book, congratulations! You've got your rhythm chops happening! To be a solid all-around musician, regardless of style, it's a good idea to know how to build chords. By learning a few basic formulas, you will be able to teach yourself any chord you can think of. You will also be able to name any chord that you can play. It's really no more difficult than balancing your checkbook! (Well, maybe that's not such a good example, but if you can make it through this chapter you should be in good shape.)

Most chords will belong to one of the following three categories: Major, Minor, or Dominant. Although these three are the most common, there are many others:

Diminished
Half diminished (m7♭5)
Augmented
Suspended or "sus"
Altered
And of course, the "other" category: power chords, slash chords, etc.

The first and most important thing you must know is: *All of the formulas for building chords are going to be based on the major scale.* Here's how it works: First, each scale step is given a number.

C major scale

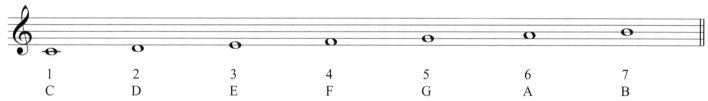

1	2	3	4	5	6	7
C	D	E	F	G	A	B

Now to build chords, we simply follow the numbers.

Major

Chord	Type	Formula	Notes
C	major triad	1–3–5	C–E–G
C6	major 6	1–3–5–6	C–E–G–A
Cma7	major 7	1–3–5–7	C–E–G–B

Are you with me so far? OK, let's move on to some major chords with *extensions*. When we arrive at C eight steps higher from where we started, this is known as an *octave*. If we continue above the octave, the following three extensions are possible:

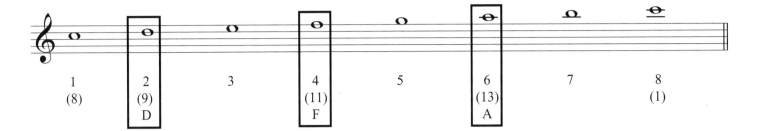

	1	2	3	4	5	6	7	8
	(8)	(9)		(11)		(13)		(1)
		D		F		A		

Note: Extensions remain the same regardless of the chord type. For example, the 9th of a C chord is D regardless of whether the C chord is major, minor, or dominant. There is no extension for the 1, 3, 5, or 7.

As most of us do not have more than five fingers on each hand, sometimes we have to leave notes out of extended chords. For some of the longer chords, I've underlined the notes necessary to name the chord.

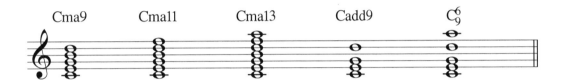

Chord	Type	Formula	Notes
Cma9	major 9	1–3–5–7–9	C–E–G–B–D
Cma11	major 11*	1–3–5–7–9–11	C–E–G–B–D–F
Cma13	major 13	1–3–5–7–9–11–13	C–E–G–B–D–F–A
Cma(add9)	major add9**	1–3–5–9	C–E–G–D
C6/9	6/9	1–3–5–6–9	C–E–G–A–D

* Although in theory this is the correct formula for a major 11 chord, the 11 is rarely used in a chord with a major 3rd present. This is because of the dissonance created by the half step interval between the major 3rd and the 11 (same pitch as 4). Instead, the 11 is usually raised a half step, making the chord a #11.

** When a triad contains an extension, but no 7th, simply name the triad ("C" for example) and then describe the extension using the word "add." For example, Cma(add9) indicates a C major triad with an added 9th.

Minor

If we take the 3rd of a major chord and lower it by one half step (one fret), the resulting chord is minor. The lowered note is called a "flat" and is written (♭). Notice also that the 7 is lowered in a minor 7 chord.

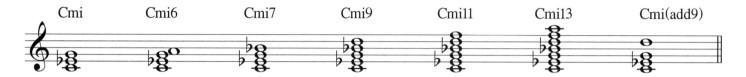

Chord	Type	Formula	Notes
Cmi	minor triad	1–♭3–5	C–E♭–G
Cmi6	minor 6	1–♭3–5–6	C–E♭–G–A
Cmi7	minor 7	1–♭3–5–♭7	C–E♭–G–B♭
Cmi9	minor 9	1–♭3–5–♭7–9	C–E♭–G–B♭–D
Cmi11	minor 11	1–♭3–5–♭7–9–11	C–E♭–G–B♭–D–F
Cmi13	minor 13	1–♭3–5–♭7–9–11–13	C–E♭–G–B♭–D–F–A
Cmi(add9)	minor add9	1–♭3–5–9	C–E♭–G–D

Dominant

The dominant chord requires four notes. It should have a major 3rd and a ♭7th.

Chord	Type	Formula	Notes
C7	dom 7	1–3–5–♭7	C–E–G–B♭
C9	dom 9	1–3–5–♭7–9	C–E–G–B♭–D
C11	dom 11	1–3–5–♭7–9–11	C–E–G–B♭–D–F
C13	dom 13	1–3–5–♭7–9–11–13	C–E–G–B♭–D–F–A

Diminished

The diminished 7th chord is interesting because it is symmetrical. When you move up or down any three frets, the chord has exactly the same notes, only in a different order. Try it out! (Note: This does not work with a diminished triad—only a diminished 7th chord.)

Chord	Type	Formula	Notes
C°	diminished triad	1–♭3–♭5	C–E♭–G♭
C°7	diminished 7th	1–♭3–♭5–♭♭7	C–E♭–G♭-B♭♭

Minor 7♭5

Also known as "half diminished," the minor 7♭5 chord is the VII chord in the major scale.

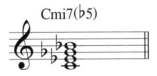

Chord	Type	Formula	Notes
Cmi7(♭5)	minor 7♭5	1–♭3–♭5–♭7	C–E♭–G♭–B♭

Augmented

If a scale step is raised one half step, it is called a sharp (♯) and is written in front of the scale step number.

Chord	Type	Formula	Notes
C+	augmented triad	1–3–♯5	C–E–G♯
C+7	augmented 7 (7#5)	1–3–♯5–♭7	C–E–G♯–B♭

Suspended

These chords are neither major or minor because they have no 3rd.

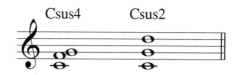

Chord	Type	Formula	Notes
Csus4	sus4	1–4–5	C–F–G
Csus2	sus2*	1–2–5	C–D–G

*The sus2 chord can also be called a sus9 chord, or a power add 2 chord (5/2)

Altered

If an extension (9, 11, or 13) is raised (♯) or lowered (♭), it is called an *alteration*. Alterations are quite often done to dominant chords. There are lots of combinations, so here are a few:

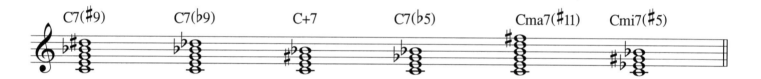

Chord	Type	Formula	Notes
C7(♯9)	7♯9	1–3–5–♭7–♯9	C–E–G–B♭–D♯
C7(♭9)	7♭9	1–3–5–♭7–♭9	C–E–G–B♭–D♭
C7(♯5)	7♯5	1–3–♯5–♭7	C–E–G♯–B♭
C7(♭5)	7♭5	1–3–♭5–♭7	C–E–G♭–B♭
C7(♯9♭5)	7♯9♭5	1–3–♭5–♭7–♯9	C–E–G♭–B♭–D♯

Alterations can also be done to major or minor chords. Here are a few:

Chord	Type	Formula	Notes
Cma7(♯11)	major 7#11	1–3–5–7–9–#11	C–E–G–B–D–F#
Cmi7(♯5)	minor 7#5	1–♭3–#5–♭7	C–E♭–G♯–B♭

Other Chords

A *power chord* has two notes: the root (1) and the 5th.

A *slash chord* is a chord with a note other than root (1) in the bass. The first letter to the left is the chord (usually a triad); the note written to the right is the bass note. For example, C/A indicates a C triad with A in the bass.

A *polychord* occurs when two chords are played simultaneously. This is more common on the piano!

The *minor major 7* chord is exactly what it says it is—a minor triad with a major 7!

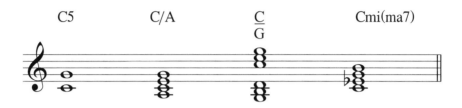

Chord	Type	Formula	Notes
C5	power chord	1–5	C–G
C/A	slash chord	1–3–5/6	C–E–G/ A
$\frac{C}{G}$	polychord	1–3–5	C–E–G–B–D
Cmi(ma7)	minor major 7	1–♭3–5–7	C–E♭–G–B

Keep in mind that there is almost always more than one way to name a chord. Sometimes, it may be easier to name a chord as a slash chord or even as a polychord. The combinations are endless! The number of chords and the ways they can be played are limited only by your imagination. This is by no means a list of all chords!! These are just some of the few I've encountered. Add your own to this short list.

Quiz

Now it's time to test yourself. To build any chord, simply do what the chord tells you! Name the formulas for the following chords. Don't cheat!

1. 7(♯9)

2. 7(♭9)

3. ma7(♯11)

4. mi(ma7)

5. add9(♯11)

Answers

1. 7(♯9): 1–3–5–♭7–♯9. Also known as the Hendrix chord. Here's how I would go about figuring this out:

   a) A 7th chord which does not specify major or minor is a dominant chord: 1–3–5–♭7

   b) Add the extension ♯9

   c) The chord formula would be: 1–3–5–♭7–♯9

2. 7(♭9): 1–3–5–♭7–♭9

   a) Once again a dominant chord: 1–3–5–♭7

   b) Add the ♭9

   c) The formula is: 1–3–5–♭7–♭9

3. ma7(♯11): 1–3–5–7–9–♯11

   a) A major 7 chord: 1–3–5–7

   b) Add the extensions 9 and ♯11

   c) The formula is 1–3–5–7–9–♯11

   d) The necessary notes are 3–7–♯11

4. mi(ma7): 1–♭3–5–7

   a) The minor triad is 1–♭3–5

   b) Add the major 7

   c) The formula is 1–♭3–5–7

5. add9(♯11): 1–5–9–♯11

   a) An add9 chord is 1–5–9

   b) Add the ♯11

What if you need to build a chord based on a note other than C? The following Transposition Chart should help. It shows the major scale degrees for just about any possible root note. Build away!

Transposition Chart

1	2(9)	3	4(11)	5	6(13)	7
C	D	E	F	G	A	B
C♯/D♭	D♯/E♭	E♯/F	F♯/G♭	G♯/A♭	A♯/B♭	B♯/C
D	E	F♯	G	A	B	C♯
D♯/E♭	E♯/F	F𝄪/G	G♯/A♭	A♯/B♭	B♯/C	C𝄪/D
E	F♯	G♯	A	B	C♯	D♯
F	G	A	B♭	C	D	E
F♯/G♭	G♯/A♭	A♯/B♭	B/C♭	C♯/D♭	D♯/E♭	E♯/F
G	A	B	C	D	E	F♯
G♯/A♭	A♯/B♭	B♯/C	C♯/D♭	D♯/E♭	E♯/F	F𝄪/G
A	B	C♯	D	E	F♯	G♯
A♯/B♭	B𝄪/C	C𝄪/D	D♯/E♭	E♯/F	F𝄪/G	G𝄪/A
B	C♯	D♯	E	F♯	G♯	A♯

Final Thoughts

Play until your fingers bleed! Improving your rhythm guitar playing will make you a better soloist and a better musician. Listen to other musicians—especially drummers. There are many places to find inspiration—music, movies, metronomes, etc. Use them all to your advantage. Perform in front of people! This will make all of your practicing worthwhile.

While there are some players that seem to be more "natural" than others, most of us (especially myself) have to work at it. Guitar playing can be a very humbling experience. You are not alone! The best solution is to always enjoy what you're doing and...play until your fingers bleed!

Danny

About the Author

Danny Gill is the co-author of MI's Rock Lead Guitar series—a complete course in soloing that includes the books *Rock Lead Basics, Rock Lead Techniques,* and *Rock Lead Performance.* He has also written the book *Practice Trax for Guitar* and is the author/performer of the videos *Rock Lead Guitar* and *Modern Rock Guitar.* Danny has also released two CD's on Universal Records with his band Speak No Evil. As a writer, his songs have appeared on numerous network TV shows and major motion picture soundtracks. At MI, Danny has taught rock lead guitar, rock rhythm guitar, single-string technique, rhythm guitar, and various live performance workshops.

Musicians Institute Press

is the official series of Southern California's renowned music school, Musicians Institute. **MI** instructors, some of the finest musicians in the world, share their vast knowledge and experience with you – no matter what your current level. For guitar, bass, drums, vocals, and keyboards, **MI Press** offers the finest music curriculum for higher learning through a variety of series:

ESSENTIAL CONCEPTS
Designed from MI core curriculum programs.

MASTER CLASS
Designed from MI elective courses.

PRIVATE LESSONS
Tackle a variety of topics "one-on-one" with MI faculty instructors.

BASS

Arpeggios for Bass
by Dave Keif • **Private Lessons**
00695133 .... $12.95

The Art of Walking Bass
A Method for Acoustic or Electric Bass
by Bob Magnusson • **Master Class**
00695168 Book/CD Pack.................. $17.95

Bass Fretboard Basics
by Paul Farnen • **Essential Concepts**
00695201 .... $12.95

Bass Playing Techniques
by Alexis Sklarevski • **Essential Concepts**
00695207 .... $16.95

Grooves for Electric Bass
by David Keif • **Private Lessons**
00695265 Book/CD Pack.................. $14.95

Latin Bass
The Essential Guide to Afro-Cuban and Brazilian Styles
by George Lopez and David Keif • **Private Lessons**
00695543 Book/CD Pack.................. $14.95

Music Reading for Bass
by Wendy Wrehovcsik • **Essential Concepts**
00695203 .... $10.95

Odd-Meter Bassics
by Dino Monoxelos • **Private Lessons**
00695170 Book/CD Pack.................. $14.95

GUITAR

Advanced Scale Concepts & Licks for Guitar
by Jean Marc Belkadi • **Private Lessons**
00695298 Book/CD Pack $14.95

Advanced Guitar Soloing
By Daniel Gilbert & Beth Marlis • **Essential Concepts**
00695636 Book/CD Pack.................. $19.95

Basic Blues Guitar
by Steve Trovato • **Private Lessons**
00695180 Book/CD Pack.................. $14.95

Classical & Fingerstyle Guitar Techniques
by David Oakes • **Master Class**
00695171 Book/CD Pack.................. $14.95

Contemporary Acoustic Guitar
by Eric Paschal & Steve Trovato • **Master Class**
00695320 Book/CD Pack.................. $16.95

Creative Chord Shapes
by Jamie Findlay • **Private Lessons**
00695172 Book/CD Pack.................. $9.95

Diminished Scale for Guitar
by Jean Marc Belkadi • **Private Lessons**
00695227 Book/CD Pack.................. $9.95

Essential Rhythm Guitar
Patterns, Progressions and Techniques for All Styles
by Steve Trovato • **Private Lessons**
00695181 Book/CD Pack.................. $14.95

Funk Guitar: The Essential Guide
by Ross Bolton • **Private Lessons**
00695419 Book/CD Pack.................. $14.95

Guitar Basics
by Bruce Buckingham • **Private Lessons**
00695134 Book/CD Pack.................. $16.95

Guitar Hanon
by Peter Deneff • **Private Lessons**
00695321 .... $9.95

Guitar Lick-tionary
By Dave HIll • **Private Lessons**
00695482 Book/CD Pack.................. $17.95

Guitar Soloing
by Dan Gilbert & Beth Marlis • **Essential Concepts**
00695190 Book/CD Pack.................. $19.95
00695638 Video $19.95

Harmonics for Guitar
by Jamie Findlay • **Private Lessons**
00695169 Book/CD Pack.................. $9.95

Jazz Guitar Chord System
by Scott Henderson • **Private Lessons**
00695291 .... $7.95

Jazz Guitar Improvisation
by Sid Jacobs • **Master Class**
00695128 Book/CD Pack.................. $17.95
00695639 Video $19.95

Jazz-Rock Triad Improvising
by Jean Marc Belkadi • **Private Lessons**
00695361 Book/CD Pack.................. $14.95

Latin Guitar
The Essential Guide to Brazilian and Afro-Cuban Rhythms
by Bruce Buckingham • **Master Class**
00695379 Book/CD Pack.................. $14.95

Modern Approach to Jazz, Rock & Fusion Guitar
by Jean Marc Belkadi • **Private Lessons**
00695143 Book/CD Pack.................. $14.95

Modes for Guitar
by Tom Kolb • **Private Lessons**
00695555 Book/CD Pack.................. $16.95

Music Reading for Guitar
by David Oakes • **Essential Concepts**
00695192 .... $16.95

The Musician's Guide to Recording Acoustic Guitar
by Dallan Beck • **Private Lessons**
00695505 Book/CD Pack.................. $12.95

Practice Trax for Guitar
by Danny Gill • **Private Lessons**
00695601 Book/CD Pack.................. $14.95

Rhythm Guitar
by Bruce Buckingham & Eric Paschal • **Essential Concepts**
00695188 Book......................... $16.95
00695644 Video $19.95

Rock Lead Basics
by Nick Nolan & Danny Gill • **Master Class**
00695144 Book/CD Pack.................. $15.95
00695637 Video $19.95

Rock Lead Performance
by Nick Nolan & Danny Gill • **Master Class**
00695278 Book/CD Pack.................. $16.95

Rock Lead Techniques
by Nick Nolan & Danny Gill • **Master Class**
00695146 Book/CD Pack.................. $15.95

Slap & Pop Technique For Guitar
00695645 Book/CD Pack.................. $12.95

Texas Blues Guitar
by Robert Calva • **Private Lessons**
00695340 Book/CD Pack.................. $16.95

FOR MORE INFORMATION, SEE YOUR LOCAL MUSIC DEALER, OR WRITE TO:

HAL•LEONARD®
CORPORATION
7777 W. BLUEMOUND RD. P.O.BOX 13819 MILWAUKEE, WI 53213

Visit Hal Leonard Online at **www.halleonard.com**